KU-647-390

CONTENTS

WHO THIS KIT IS FOR

The *StartUp Kit* is for anyone considering or starting a business.

You may have been thinking about how you can make a living from a particular passion, hobby or skill. Perhaps you're working a day job and already making sales on the side — now you want to take it to the next level. Maybe you haven't hit upon the right idea yet; you just know in your heart that you want to be your own boss.

This kit offers all the tools, tips and templates you need to succeed. It'll help you find an idea, spot a gap in the market and start your own small business. Doing so will be one of the best moves you've ever made!

ABOUT THE AUTHOR

Emma Jones is a business expert, author and founder of small business community Enterprise Nation. Her books include *Working 5 to 9*, *Go Global: How to take your business to the world* and *Turn Your Talent Into a Business*.

Following a five-year career at an international accounting firm, Emma started her first business at 27. That business was sold 18 months later, and the experience led to Emma's next venture, Enterprise Nation.

Its website (**www.enterprisenation.com**) was launched in 2006 and became the most popular site for home business owners in the UK, attracting over 100,000 visitors each month.

In seven years, Enterprise Nation has grown into a community of over 75,000 homegrown businesses that find help and support on its website, in its books and at live events. In 2011, the company gave away over £10,000 in funding to UK start-ups, and has recently launched a premium membership scheme, which helps its members promote their businesses and take their venture to the next level.

Emma is also a co-founder of StartUp Britain, a national campaign to encourage more people to start a business.

Emma was awarded an MBE for services to enterprise in July 2012.

66 There is a satisfaction in creating your own enterprise that is unknown to those who work for others. **99**

– Lord Young of Graffham

FOREWORD
BY LORD YOUNG OF GRAFFHAM

As a serial entrepreneur and an occasional politician I have seen how enterprise changes people's lives, including my own. I often boast that I haven't worked since March 1961, when I left my then-employer and set up my first business. Of course, working for yourself is not always fun – it can be hard, often lonely, not always successful – but at the end of the day there is a satisfaction in creating your own enterprise that is unknown to those who work for others.

And this is not just a selfish interest. Our economy today is made up of many millions – four and a half million to be exact – of small firms, of which over a million were created in the last decade. I believe that another million will be created over the next ten years and yours could be one of them.

Some 30 years ago I created the very first business start-up programme. Some of the companies that started all those years ago are amongst the biggest in the land; but the vast majority are still small firms that have provided a lifetime's income for their founders. More recently, I launched the StartUp Loan (www.startuploans.co.uk) programme that is designed to help anyone aged 18 to 24 create a business plan and then get a loan to get started, as well as benefit from mentor support.

I believe the opportunity to meet a mentor, to talk through a possible business plan, to appreciate what is required to start, will benefit nearly all who go through the process. The limits of your business will then be up to you.

This kit is your first step to your new life. Read it and take advantage of all it offers. From this moment onwards, a new door opens.

LORD YOUNG OF GRAFFHAM | @THELORDYOUNG

Lord Young is Enterprise Adviser to the Prime Minister

66 In this kit, I'll show you how to start and grow a successful business in your spare time, from home and on a budget. 99

LET'S GET STARTED

There has never been a better time to start a business and in 2012 record numbers of people did just that. A survey called the Global Entrepreneurship Monitor revealed the highest number of people starting a business since research began in 1999. This was closely followed by data from the Department for Business, Innovation and Skills showing the number of small businesses having increased to 4.8 million at the start of 2012 – a record high.

Why is this happening? Simple: because it's now perfectly possible to start and grow a successful business

- in your spare time
- from home
- on a budget
- with help from friends and others.

In this kit, I'll show you how it's done.

People in their thousands are spotting gaps in the market or turning their hobbies into a successful venture. They are embracing free or low-cost technology to promote themselves and make sales, with a good number of these sales coming from overseas customers. Having access to the internet means you can start a business on a Monday and be trading with the world by Wednesday.

The start-up companies profiled in this book discuss how they got going and how they accessed the invaluable support that's helped them along the way. They are selling everything from apple jams to iPhone apps, cushions to cakes, and high-end Italian fashion. Their products may be different, but the owners of these businesses all talk about the opportunities available to them and the joy of having the freedom to work how and where they like. They are of all ages. Many started in employment. A good number are already going global.

If you'd like to experience the same sense of independence and excitement, all you have to do is follow some basic steps: come up with an idea, do some research and marketing, offer good customer service – and you're in business!

In the following pages I'll walk you through everything that's involved in doing this successfully.

EMMA JONES | @EMMALJONES

ClubWorkspace
Network. Collaborate. Innovate.

moo.com

ΙΝΤUΙΤ.

oDesk

PayPal™

Regus

HOW TO ACCESS YOUR OFFERS

The StartUp Kit comes with a range of offers from top brands. These deals are on everything from a website to a virtual office, business cards and accounting software. They are ideal for your new start-up.

To find out more about the offers available, and to take advantage of them, head to:

www.enterprisenation.com/startupkit2013

Here you'll find details of all partner offers. To access these simply enter the code below, select the individual offers you want, and you'll be shown the links and offer codes you need.

You don't have to access all the offers at once if you don't want to; you can come back at any time.

We'll be adding new offers throughout the year and you'll be able to access those too.

ACCESS CODE: supk13

And that's not all ...

As well as accessing the partner offers, you can also use the above link to download templates, get hold of resources and stay bang up-to-date on the latest small business news!

eBook edition

You can download an eBook edition of this kit to read on the go on your smartphone, laptop or Kindle. Simply head to **www.enterprisenation.com/startupkit2013** above or snap the QR code here.

I. PREPARE

With any undertaking, preparation is key. Whether baking a cake, going on a date or heading on holiday, time is given over to research and preparation. Starting a business is no different. Dedicate time to coming up with an idea, ensuring it's viable, and registering with the relevant bodies. These are the base ingredients required for a successful enterprise!

1. COMING UP WITH AN IDEA

Ingredient number one: a business idea! Many people tell me they would like to start a business but what's holding them back is not having an idea. It's easy to come up with one. Ask yourself these three questions:

1. Is there a gap in the market?

Have you tried to buy something that you just can't find? Could others be looking for the same thing? If so, this presents a market opportunity. Louise Doyle (page 4) spotted a gap in the market when friend and now co-founder, Carole Loader, complained about the lack of a piece of software that could make life easier. Seeing that people might be interested in such a product, Louise's own business was born.

2. What is my passion/hobby/skill?

Many people are turning what they love into a way of making a living. Best of all, when you work on what you enjoy, doing it never really feels like work. Are you a dab hand at design? Have an eye for photography? A head for figures? These skills and hobbies can easily be turned into a business.

3. Is there something someone else is doing that I can do better myself?

If you've bought something and been unimpressed, why not step in, set up a business, and provide a better offer? Many good ideas stem from spotting products and services that can simply be improved upon or offered for less.

* * *

Your idea will develop over time. Don't be surprised if in 12 months' time it looks different to when you started out. This is okay. Business ideas tend to get refined over time; your offer will get sharper the more experience you gain in the marketplace. What's important is to get started with the beginnings of an idea – there'll be time to develop it as you get feedback from customers and input from others.

CASE STUDY

The idea for Louise Doyle's business came about when Carole Loader (her subsequent co-founder) was describing the pain of self-assessment with the training provider for which she worked. Carole wondered why a company hadn't built a piece of software to make quality-improvement planning easier.

With her own background as director of a college, Louise immediately knew the idea had potential and that Carole had spotted a gap in the market.

"After some initial research I called Neil Donkin with whom I'd previously worked to ask if he would build a prototype. The three of us formed a team."

Louise and her fellow founders came to the business in different ways. Mesma is Carole's first experience of being her own boss after being employed in the government-funded training sector for most of her career. Neil had always worked on a freelance basis but at the time of setting up Mesma was (and still is) employed by a large qualifications awarding body. Louise had run her own education consultancy business since 2009 to give her flexibility after having children, and she had her eyes open for a business with greater growth potential when the time was right.

The company began trading in February 2012 after an eight month test-and-development period. The team gained their first client by giving them a free trial of the software, securing both a development partner and a client. "Their feedback was invaluable to help us iron out some early usability issues," says Louise.

Access to the education sector was relatively straightforward for this team of three as they had contacts and experience in the sector. To promote the company, Mesma has delivered free webinars, used an external appointment-setting company during peak sales periods, worked with membership organisations to help spread the story to a wider network, and utilised social media and networking to interact with potential clients. "We use a number of marketing channels, none of which cost us huge amounts of money because we don't have it!"

The directors work well together and, not being in the same space each day, means making the most of technology to keep in touch with daily phone calls and email, weekly web meetings and monthly detailed board meetings.

Employing staff and apprentices is just one aspect of the growth plan for this business as the founders commit to increasing sales in the further education market in the UK whilst also exploring international markets.

- www.mesma.co.uk | @MesmaUK

TOP TIP: "Our success as a partnership to date is based on our fierce ambition for our business, the values we share and the fact that each of us brings different experience and skills."

50 ideas for businesses

These are all ideas and businesses we have seen and profiled on Enterprise Nation. Many of them started as '5 to 9' businesses. In other words, a business started whilst the entrepreneur was in full-time study or employment. More on that later!

Blogger
Vlogger
Social media advisor
eBay trader
Online store owner
Giftware maker
Giftware seller
Artisan
Cupcake maker
Cosmetics producer
Hair and make-up artist
Origami artist
Picture artist
Furniture marker
Jewellery designer
Footwear designer
Fashion designer

Clothing producer
Toymaker
Party organiser
DJ
Musician
Magician
Beer producer
Events organiser
Wedding planner
Mystery shopper
Image consultant
Fitness advisor
Personal trainer
Photographer
Accountant
Lawyer

Translator
IT services
App developer
Software developer
Print and web designer
Network marketer
Pet care
Product manufacturer
E-learning provider
Facebook developer
Magazine publisher
T-shirt maker
Papercrafter
Dance instructor
Perfumer
Balloon decorator
Street advertiser

There are so many possibilities. You might even have too many ideas. In which case, don't be afraid to spend some time on all of them and, wherever possible, let the customer decide – try them out in small ways and see what gets the warmest response.

Niche is nice

When coming up with your idea, bear in mind that niche businesses are often ideal. Meeting the needs of a very well-defined audience helps keep your efforts focused and your offering clear in a crowded market. It also means success should naturally consolidate itself. So rather than just selling clothes, why not become the go-to place for men's blazers (page 103), and instead of offering food to suit all palates, how about re-inventing pizza so it offers a balanced meal to consumers interested in healthy eating (p.101)?

With a niche business:

- **you keep marketing costs low**, as your audience is well-defined; you know where your audience are and understand the kind of marketing messages to which they will respond

- **customer loyalty remains high**, as you become the expert in your field or the only provider of certain products; customers will want to stay with you and benefit from the specialist product or service you offer.

FRIENDS AND FAMILY FOCUS GROUP: Talk to family and friends and ask them where they think your talents lie. They might just help you discover your business idea in an area you hadn't thought of.

The niche list

Here are some businesses I've come across that have benefited from having a clear niche. A few of them are profiled in this guide:

- Collie Wobbles (www.colliewobbles.co.uk) | *Border Collie/sheepdog-related products*

- Rock 'n' Roll Bride (www.rocknrollbride.com) | *For brides wanting a rock 'n' roll wedding*

- WorkSnug (www.worksnug.com) | *For mobile workers seeking connected spaces*

- Cambridge Raincoat Company (www.cambridgeraincoats.co.uk) | *Fashion raincoats for people who ride upright bicycles*
- Peach Blossom (www.peachblossom.co.uk) | *Stylish party products for the stylish party host*
- Bird and Bumble (www.birdandbumble.com) | *A site for food suppliers and lovers across London*

* * *

Whatever the idea, good ones tend be based on what you enjoy, what people will buy and something that improves on what's already available. Think about how you can fashion your idea so it has a clear purpose for a clearly defined audience.

Use this template to help come up with your idea:

Template 1: What's the Big Idea?

Have I spotted a gap in the market?

What is my passion/hobby/skill?

Is there something I've seen that I can do better myself?

What about buying into someone else's idea via a franchise?

An idea as part of the package

If you're not able to settle on a viable idea of your own, consider buying into someone else's idea. You can do so through a franchise or signing up as a party-plan consultant and/or direct sales agent. Benefit from being your own boss whilst having the support of a central team and the proven idea that comes with it!

Here are 20 top franchise or party-plan opportunities (from *50 Fantastic Franchises!*, Brightword Publishing, 2011).

- My Secret Kitchen | www.mysecretkitchen.co.uk
- Jamie at Home | www.jamieathome.com
- The Pampered Chef | www.pamperedchef.co.uk
- Girlie Gardening | www.girliegardening.com
- Avon | www.avon.uk.com
- Kleeneze | www.kleeneze.com
- Neal's Yard | www.nealsyardremedies.com
- Maid2Clean | www.maid2clean.co.uk
- Razzamataz | www.razzamataz.co.uk

- Harmony At Home | www.harmonyathome.co.uk

- Shoes Glorious Shoes | www.shoesgloriousshoes.co.uk

- Travel Counsellors | www.travelcounsellors.co.uk

- Tatty Bumpkin | www.tattybumpkin.com

- Barrett & Coe | www.barrettandcoe.co.uk

- Barking Mad | www.barkingmad.uk.com

- Curves | www.curves.co.uk

- Spanish Amigos www.spanishamigos.co.uk

- PyjamaDrama | www.pyjamadrama.com

- Usborne Books | www.usborne.com

- Captain Tortue Group | www.captaintortuegroup.com

USEFUL LINKS

- Direct Selling Association | www.dsa.org.uk

- British Franchise Association | www.thebfa.org

- *50 Fantastic Franchises!* eBook | www.brightwordpublishing.com

" Choose a business idea that you are passionate about. You're going to be spending a lot of time on it. And when you're working on something you love, it stops being work and feels more like fun. "

– Michael Acton-Smith,
founder, Moshi Monsters

2. RESEARCH THE MARKET

You have your idea. Turning it into a business requires some research, followed by a straightforward exercise in building that research into a plan. Here's how to go about it.

First, **research your potential customers**, the competition and a price point by visiting competitors' sites, online trade sites/forums, reading reports, and seeking intelligence from experts.

Look for data and comments that will answer the following questions:

- What is the number of potential customers you can serve, and how do these customers like to be served?
- What are their core characteristics and spending patterns, and who are their key influencers?
- Who is currently serving your market?
- Where are your potential customers going for their goods and services?
- What do they like about what they're getting and, more importantly, what do they dislike (as this opens up opportunities for you to improve on the status quo)?

In view of the above, what price can you charge for your product/service?

Price yourself at a rate that's competitive with other providers in the market, that takes into account the amount of time, personal service and added value you offer, and that will turn a profit at the end of the day.

WHAT AM I WORTH? How much do you think customers or clients would pay for your product or service? Take a look at how similar offerings are priced and talk to people about how much they'd be willing to pay. Then talk to suppliers to check you can source materials and deliver at a price that covers your costs. Since starting a business from home (which I recommend you do!) will save you lots of money, you can pass some of these savings onto your customers. It will give you an edge over other businesses. But don't undercharge for the expertise and knowledge you offer. Only consider charging less for work that will reflect well on your business and boost your reputation, perhaps in the media or with a particularly important customer.

You can also source primary, or firsthand, data by conducting a survey or posing questions on social media channels.

Survey tools

- SurveyMonkey | www.surveymonkey.com
- Wufoo | www.wufoo.com

Social media channels

- Twitter | www.twitter.com
- Facebook | www.facebook.com
- LinkedIn | www.linkedin.com

Or, of course, you can hit the streets with a clipboard! Work on your own market research plan by completing Template 2.

The name game

Coming up with an idea and carrying out research will get you thinking about what to name your business. If selling your knowledge, the company could be named after you – for example, 'Emma Jones Advisory Services'. In which case, job done! But if you're looking for something else, think of a name that:

- is easy to spell
- has an available domain name
- is not already registered with Companies House (use the free web-check service to access existing company names at www.companieshouse.gov.uk)
- people will remember.

You might want to protect the name with a trademark. See page 29 for information on how to go about that.

If you get stuck, visit Enterprise Nation (www.enterprisenation.com) where you will find people who can help you: the site is buzzing with talented copywriters and wordsmiths.

Template 2: Market Research

How big is the market?

What is the number of potential customers I can serve and how do these customers like to be served?

What are their characteristics, spending patterns and who are their key influences?

Who is currently serving my market?

Where are my potential customers going for their goods and services?

What do they like about what they're getting, and, more importantly, what do they dislike?

What price can I charge for my product/service?

What's competitive and takes into account the amount of time, personal service and added value that I offer?

SWOT analysis

With your idea, and now your research in-hand that supports it, prepare a SWOT analysis. This stands for: **S**trengths, **W**eaknesses, **O**pportunities, **T**hreats and looks as follows:

Strengths

What are my strengths?

What can I do better than anyone else?

What resources do I have?

What's my unique selling point?

Weaknesses

What are my weaknesses?

What should I avoid?

Where do I lack skills?

What might hinder my success?

Opportunities

What opportunities do I see?

Does my idea tap into any trends?

Are there any emerging technologies that could help my idea?

Has there been anything in the news related to my idea?

Threats

What threats might I face?

Who's my competition?

Does changing technology affect my idea?

Template 3: SWOT Analysis

Strengths

What are my strengths?

Weaknesses

What are my weaknesses?

Opportunities

What opportunities do I see?

Threats

What threats might I face?

3. WRITE A PLAN

A business plan will act as your map. It will guide the business from start to growth, with reference to milestones along the way.

The plan will include information about how you intend to get started and what your ultimate objectives are – and how you aim to get from one to the other. You might want to start a business and sell it in a few years' time, or grow to a point where you wouldn't want to grow anymore.

Of course, you'll need to refer to resources: what you have already, what you'll need and how you'll pay for it.

So, after coming up with an idea and doing your research, writing the business plan is your first practical step to starting your business. With it under your belt you can say, "I'm off!"

Or IMOFF. It's an easy way to remember the headings to include in your business plan: **I**dea, **M**arket, **O**perations, **F**inancials and **F**riends. Have these as headings in your plan and you've taken a big step closer to becoming your own boss.

Idea

What's your idea?

Market

Who will be your customers or clients? And who is your competition?

Operations

How will you develop the idea, promote it and provide good customer service?

Financials

Can you earn more than you spend, so that the business makes a profit? Do you need any funds to get started?

Friends

Do you have a support network on hand for when you need business advice? Are there complementary businesses you've identified with whom partnerships are a possibility?

Return regularly to your plan to check progress against targets or to make amends as you respond to new opportunities.

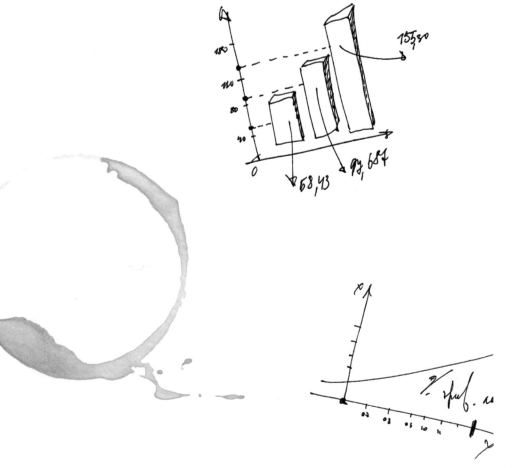

Executive Summary

Summarise what's in the rest of the plan. Something like this:

The vision for ABC is to become the leading company for selling *abc* to *xyz*. This plan sets out how the vision will be achieved in the period 2013-2015. It outlines the product on offer, provides data on the market and shows how the company will be operating profitably within the first three months.

Having identified a clear gap in the market, I'm excited about the opportunity to start and build a successful business that will offer a quality product [or service] to a well-defined market.

A. Person
Founder, Company ABC

The Idea

Include here your 'elevator pitch'; what is your product and how will it benefit the customer?

This is the opportunity to explain the idea of the business in a few sentences.

* This title would be more like 'Advisory Board' if preparing the plan for a bank or funder.

The Market

Customers
Who will be your customers? Include the quantity, their demographic profile, geographic locations, social backgrounds; essentially any strong data that shows you know your audience.

Competition
Who is selling a similar product/service? How do you differ from them? What is your unique selling point?

You can do this by producing a table that lists the competition. Outline what makes you stand out in the market: is it that your service will be online, that you'll charge a different price, have an innovative marketing approach or offer the service with a special extra twist?

Operations

The CEO
You have come up with the idea for the business and you've done your research on the market. Now it's time for the reader to know a bit about you! Note your background, skills, experience and any credentials for running this business. Plus information on other key members of staff (if there are any).

Sourcing
If this applies to your business, refer to how you'll source your product/service. You may be making it yourself!

Sales & Marketing

How will you promote what you offer to your customers? Include a brief sales and marketing plan with headings like this:

Press – how many press releases do you plan to distribute each year and to which press channels: newspapers, magazines, radio, etc.?

Online – will you have your own blog/website? Mention other sites that you'll approach for reciprocal links.

Partners – what about marketing tie-ups with other companies selling to the same audience?

You know where your customers are, so let your marketing plan show that you'll reach them in print, online and even in the streets!

Systems

You've sourced the service/product and told customers about it. Refer here to the process customers will go through to buy from you and the systems you'll have in place to deliver in time and on budget. Systems that may include online ordering and payment, a professional call-handling service to take orders or maybe some specific software.

Financials

Last but not least come the figures. Make this as clear as possible and it's probably best to do it in table form:

	Year 1	Year 2
Revenue		
Overheads		
Office rent		
Salary		
Stock		
Technology		
Marketing		
Travel & expenses		
Projected profit		

Drawing up a simple financial forecast will highlight any need to borrow money.

Friends & Family

In starting and growing your business, will you call on friends and family for advice? If so, refer to this here; mention your board of advisors, your experts-on-call, your support network!

(See page 158 onwards for details on how to access expert advisors and find a mentor whose details you can also include here.)

Template 4: Business Plan

Use this template to write your own business plan.

Executive Summary

The Idea

The Market
Customers

Competition

Operations
The CEO

Sourcing

Sales & Marketing
Press

Online

Partners

Systems

Friends & Family

Financials

4. REGISTER THE COMPANY

When you set up in business, there are a couple of organisations you need to contact: Companies House and HM Revenue & Customs (HMRC). Before registering with either, have a think about the company status that suits you best.

Self-employed

This status means you are working for yourself. You keep records and accounts of your own activities and, in acting alone, get to keep all the profits – but are also solely liable for any debts.

Limited company

Limited companies exist in their own right, with the company's finances kept separate from the personal finances of its owners, so your liability is limited.

Partnership

If you'd like to be self-employed but want to work with a friend or colleague, consider a partnership. It means that two or more people share the risks, costs and workload.

Many of the companies featured in the following pages have formed a partnership. They all comment on how a mix of skills and experience is helping the business to grow.

Clippy McKenna even managed to persuade her fiancé to give up a well-paid job to help her grow her dream business . . .

CASE STUDY

NAME: **Clippy McKenna** | BUSINESS: **Clippy's**

Starting in 2008 with produce from two apple trees in her back garden and a fascination for hairclips (hence the name!) Clippy McKenna has gone on to grow a highly successful conserve, relish, chutney and savoury herb jellies business with a little help from her fiancé Paul.

"When I told my fiancé that I wanted to create a food brand focused on injecting innovation and personality into traditional food categories – starting with British apple-based jams and chutneys – he advised me to put together a business plan and secure a high profile account. Once I had completed these tasks I persuaded him to give up his well-paid job to help me build the business!"

Clippy made her first sale at Ashton-under-Lyne farmers' market. From there she secured deals with several farm shops and independent retailers, before winning a contract to supply all Harvey Nichols stores in the UK.

"In 2010 we approached Ocado with our products based on British apples and they became a customer. Then in 2011 we won deals nationally with Tesco, some Asda stores in the northwest, and E.H. Booths. Finally, in 2012 we achieved a national account with Morrisons for a brand new product called marmachilli. We also export to China and the USA."

This has all been achieved by Clippy and Paul self-funding the business together, keeping overheads low as they grow the company.

"We're a small company with big ambitions and you have to play to your strengths to succeed in the retail environment. I'm an everyday mum, who happened to love apples enough to make a business from them; I firmly believe that this original passion has helped us to promote the Clippy's brand."

The company has recently taken part in a government-funded growth accelerator programme which has helped the business yet further.

"Our coach on the programme was amazing – and a taskmaster. He helped us think about how we could grow our business to supply the supermarkets. This had a profound effect on our business. Without the help of the programme, we wouldn't be where we are today."

Clippy and Paul are now working on a complementary range of products, launching in 2013. The new range will help raise consumer awareness of Clippy's in other categories within the supermarkets. There are also plans to strengthen international expansion by working with export distributors.

"We're always thinking and planning ahead . . . it's what makes for a great business and a great partnership!"

- **www.clippys.com** | @clippysworld

See page 151 for details on how to form a partnership agreement.

See page 151 for details on how to form a partnership agreement.

IF YOU'RE UNSURE, ASK: The status of your company will affect how much admin you have to do and the kind of financial records that you need to keep and file. Take advice from your accountant or local tax office on which one to choose.

Being social

Should you decide to start a social enterprise – a business trading for social and environmental purposes – there are additional legal structures to consider, including:

- community interest company (CIC)
- industrial and provident society
- charitable status.

To find out more about launching a social enterprise or creating a CIC visit:

- Social Enterprise UK | **www.socialenterprise.org.uk**
- CIC Regulator | **www.cicregulator.gov.uk**
- 'Setting up a social enterprise' via GOV.UK | **www.gov.uk/set-up-a-social-enterprise**

Companies House

When registering with Companies House, there are three options from which to choose. You can buy a ready-made company from a company formation agent, incorporate a company yourself by sending documents and a registration fee to Companies House or register online via GOV.UK. If you decide to complete registration yourself, see form INo1 – application to register a company. It can be easier to go with a formation agent as they do the work on your behalf.

- **GOV.UK** | Incorporate via GOV.UK (www.gov.uk/register-a-company-online) and pay £15.

- **Self-incorporation** | Visit the new company registration page of the Companies House website: bit.ly/dw1xcJ. Complete form INo1. Post to Companies House with relevant fee. Standard service fee of £40 (documents processed in eight to ten days). Same-day service fee is £100.

- **Company formation agent** | Register with kit partner Companies Made Simple (www.companiesmadesimple.com). Prices start at £16.99 for standard company registration.

IN THE KIT

Companies Made Simple is a *StartUp Kit* partner, offering company formation for £16.99 and formation guaranteed in three hours.

HM Revenue & Customs

The rules on registering a new business with HM Revenue & Customs are pretty clear-cut. You are required to register as soon as you start earning from any business activity. As stated, you can choose to register as self-employed, as a partnership, or as a limited company. Each category has its own filing requirements, as shown below.

Sole trader/self-employed

The calculation of tax and National Insurance owing is done through self-assessment. You either need to complete a form CWF1, or simply call the newly self-employed business helpline. It should be done by 5 October after the end of the tax year in which you started your business to avoid a fine.

- Form CWF1 | www.hmrc.gov.uk/forms/cwf1.pdf

- Helpline for the newly self-employed | 0845 915 4515

It's not onerous to complete the form and, once registered, you'll be classified as self-employed and sent a self-assessment tax return each year, which you complete, showing your income and expenses from self-employment as well as details of your employment elsewhere (if that applies).

You will be subject to tax and National Insurance on any profits you make, but the good news is that any losses incurred can be offset against your employed income (if you have any), which could even result in a tax rebate.

Depending on your turnover and how straightforward your tax affairs are, you may be able to simply fill out the short tax return (SA200). However, this cannot be self-selected, nor is it on the HMRC website or orderable; HMRC will send it to you automatically if they think you qualify, based on information given in the previous year's return. If you have turnover below £68,000, it's likely that you will qualify. As ever, though, it will depend on individual circumstances, and the law (and various criteria it uses) may change!

Deadlines

Self-assessment tax return deadlines are as follows:

- paper tax returns should be received by HMRC by 31 October
- online tax returns should be completed by 31 January (giving you an extra three months).

Useful links

- Leaflet SE1 – 'Thinking of working for yourself?' |
  www.hmrc.gov.uk/leaflets/se1.pdf
- Helping you understand self assessment and your tax return, HMRC |
  www.hmrc.gov.uk/sa

Partnership

According to HMRC, a partnership is where:

"Two or more people set up a business. Each partner is personally responsible for all the business debts, even if the debt was caused by another partner. As partners, each pays income tax on their share of the business profits through self-assessment, as well as National Insurance."

In terms of filing requirements, each partner should complete a partnership supplementary page as part of their individual self-assessment tax return. This is in addition to a partnership return, which has to be submitted by one nominated partner and show each partner's share of profits/losses.

Deadlines

The deadlines for partnership tax returns are as follows:

- paper tax returns should be received by HMRC by 31 October

- online tax returns should be completed by 31 January (giving you an extra three months).

Limited company

Limited companies exist in their own right, with the company's finances distinct from the personal finances of the owners. What this means is that the company is liable for any debts, not the individual owners, as is the case if you are self-employed or in a partnership.

In April 2008 it became legal to form and run a limited company with just one person, without the need to involve anyone else (prior to this you also needed a company secretary). As noted, you can form a new limited company by registering with Companies House via GOV.UK (**www.gov.uk/limited-company-formation**) or by using a company creation agent.

As well as registering with Companies House, you also need to let HMRC know you are operating as a limited company. And you will need to set up and register a PAYE scheme, as you are an employee of the company.

- Register PAYE scheme | **www.hmrc.gov.uk/newemployers**

- New employer's helpline | **0845 60 70 143**

In terms of filing requirements, you should complete a self-assessment company tax return at the end of the accounting period. The return will show the company's taxable profits and whether any corporation tax is owed, and can be filed online at www.hmrc.gov.uk/ct.

The return should also be filed with Companies House to comply with the Companies Act 2006. This can be done free of charge, using the online WebFiling service at Companies House: ewf.companieshouse.gov.uk

On your returns, you can claim wear-and-tear allowances (capital allowances) on any equipment you buy, and an element of your expenses for working from home. You can also claim travelling expenses, subsistence and a proportion of your phone calls.

Deadlines

Whereas filing deadlines for self-assessment and partnership tax returns are specific dates, that is not the case with company tax returns, which must be filed 12 months after the end of your company's corporation tax accounting period.

IN GOOD ORDER: Keep records of your business dealings – this will make it much easier to complete tax returns when the time comes. Keep hold of **receipts** of business-related **purchases**; **copies of invoices** to customers; **bank statements**, especially if you don't yet have a separate account for the business (it is worth starting one); **utility bills** (if you are starting the business from home and using part of the house for business), which can be claimed as a business expense and so reduce your tax bill.

For advice from HMRC on good record keeping, visit: www.hmrc.gov.uk/startingup/keeprecs.htm

VAT

Whichever company status you choose, if your business turns over more than £77,000 (in the 2012/13 tax year), or you think your turnover will soon exceed this amount, you should also register for value added tax (VAT).

You can voluntarily register at any time. Being VAT-registered can bring credibility with certain customers, but adding VAT to your invoices may make you more expensive than competitors and you will have to file a VAT return four times a year.

- 'How and when to register for VAT', HMRC | www.hmrc.gov.uk/vat/start/register

Accountant accompaniment

Talk to a qualified accountant about the structure that is best for your business. And consider employing their services to complete your tax returns. Even if your accounts are very simple, it is well worth seeking professional advice, particularly as the rules and regulations can change frequently and without warning.

Find an accountant by visiting:

- ICAEW [Institute of Chartered Accountants for England and Wales] | **www.icaew.com**

- Accountant partners of online software tool, FreeAgent | **www.freeagent.com/partners**

Useful links

- 'Starting a Business', HMRC | **www.hmrc.gov.uk/startingup**
- 'Tax Help – and advice for small business' | **www.businesslink.gov.uk/taxhelp**

5. PROTECT THE BRAND

You have now registered with Companies House and HM Revenue & Customs. Your final consideration should be your intellectual property. You may decide to register a trademark to protect your company name or brand or, if you've come up with a unique invention, a patent. Registering either means that companies can't come along and use your name or invention without your permission.

The four forms of IP

There are four different kinds of intellectual property that you can protect:

1. Patents

These protect what makes things work. For example, says the Intellectual Property Office (IPO), "what makes a wheel turn or the chemical formula of your favourite fizzy drink".

2. Trademarks

These are "signs (like words and logos) that distinguish goods and services in the marketplace".

3. Designs

What a logo or product looks like: "from the shape of an aeroplane to a fashion item".

4. Copyright

An automatic right that comes into existence for anything written or recorded.

Register and protect your intellectual property by visiting the UK Intellectual Property Office website (**www.ipo.gov.uk**).

Charlie Ashworth is founder of Venture Proof (**www.ventureproof.com**) a company that helps small businesses protect their IP. Charlie says:

"It doesn't matter what product your business makes, or what service it provides, every enterprise is regularly generating and applying a considerable amount of intellectual property. This is a prized and valued possession – and one you should aim to protect to secure your venture."

Obi Nwosu undertook all the right measures when developing a new product that is catching on fast . . .

CASE STUDY

NAME: **Obi Nwosu** | BUSINESS: **CLICLOC London**

Obi Nwosu had held senior exec positions at internet companies such as QXL and ebookers.com when he took the decision to become his own boss and start CLICLOC London, a stylish watch company.

"I had a comfortable life, successful career and a great team but in the end the call of the start-up was too great. Even with all its challenges, I would not give up the life of an entrepreneur if I could possibly help it."

In Obi's case, the call of the start-up was for a product he'd been shown by a friend that he felt could be improved upon. The end result is CLICLOC, a range of bright and quality watches with a simple and fun design. When it came to moving from idea to business, Obi and business partner, Brian Downer, didn't waste much time.

"We had the inspiration for CLICLOC in mid 2011, and by autumn had developed our prototype. The first design, the Classic, was available to buy by November that year."

This included time required to protect the intellectual property of the product.

"During 2012 we filed trademark, design and utility patents on our products. Trademarks are the easiest to file and patents are by far the hardest. The good news is that there is a lot of information available online and with patience it is possible to get through it. I would recommend seeking specialist advice, though, especially for some parts of the patent-filing process."

With patents and trademarks filed, it was time to get the product to market and promote the company.

"We try to be as unique and exciting as possible to capture the public's imagination. This happens through our pop-up laboratories in London, product placement and media mentions on TV, online and in magazines, social media, trade and consumer shows. We experiment and take on consumers' feedback to try to determine what does and doesn't work; once we find a channel that works we focus on it. We have experimented with paid advertising but in general have not found the return worthwhile."

The two company founders have been persistent when it comes to sales and this has paid off, with a cold call leading to the Classic range of watches now being stocked in The Tate.

"We secured this deal by contacting The Tate directly – we really believe you need to be persistent and confident and just go after what you want. After a number of calls my business partner Brian got through to the right person who requested a sample. I delivered them personally and had a brief chance to chat with the buyer. Once they saw the product and we had a chance to convey our brand values they wanted to jump on board and stock the watches."

Obi and Brian make for a powerful partnership and believe one of the strengths of the partnership is in their differences:

"Our working style and strengths complement each other. I am responsible for product development, online and retailer sales and business development – it plays well to my more assertive nature, as anyone who knows me will attest. I am always thinking about new ideas, and am a passionate talker. That's important when you're pitching! Brian is responsible for our offline consumer sales and back office – he's really methodical, talented at motivating the troops and at overseeing our pop-up stalls and generally making sure things are getting done right on the ground."

The dynamic duo sell online via their own site and others – including Amazon and ASOS. They're continually monitoring the sales channels that are most effective, and thinking about how best to structure their team to get the right results.

"We'll also keep on creating! We're planning to introduce a number of new and innovative products that I've designed and patented. Innovation is important to us as it helps us continually drive sales."

● **www.clicloc.com** | **@CLICLOC** | **www.facebook.com/clicloc**

TOP TIP: "Keep moving, thinking ahead and making sure your business stays fresh and interesting."

6. TAKE CARE OF HOUSEHOLD ADMIN

When starting out, you'l likely be starting from home – your own, your parents' or maybe a friend's. It's the best way to start, keeping costs low and the commute short. In other words: more time and money for the business.

You'll probably be outsourcing work as opposed to employing staff, so there's no need for lots of people to come into the office each day. And you can meet clients and contacts in the local hotel or serviced work space. It's also good to know you're not alone in starting at home – over 60% of businesses do. You may have a few questions around household admin and who you need to tell. Here are the answers.

Q: Do I need planning permission?

A: You'll only need planning permission to base the business at home if you answer 'yes' to any of these questions:

- will your home no longer be used mainly as a private residence?
- will your business result in a marked rise in traffic or people calling?
- will your business involve any activities that are unusual in a residential area?
- will your business disturb the neighbours at unreasonable hours or create other forms of nuisance such as noise or smells?

If your house is pretty much going to remain a house, with your business quietly accommodated within it, then permission won't be required. If you're unsure, contact your local council to seek their views (**www.planningportal.gov.uk**).

Q: Do I need to tell the local authority I'm working from home?

A: Depends on whether you pass the planning test. If you need planning permission, you'll have to inform your local authority. If you don't, then the only benefit of telling them is that they'll charge you business rates (rather than council tax) on the part of the house being used for business purposes – not really much of an incentive! Business rates are different in each area and something that should be agreed with your local authority. Check out the GOV.UK guide to business rates at **www.gov.uk/introduction-to-business-rates/working-from-home**.

Q: Do I need to tell the landlord?

A: Yes, it's best to let them know that you will be working from home. Good news is, it was announced by the government on 1 November 2010 that social landlords should review any contracts prohibiting people from working from home, making it much easier for people in social housing to use living space as work space. Since then we've seen some social landlords such as London & Quadrant (**www.lqgroup.org.uk**) organise business training for tenants. A welcome sight.

Q: What about my insurance provider? Do they need to know?

A: Yes, do inform your insurance company. Tell them about the equipment and stock you have at home. An upgrade from domestic to a business policy is not expensive so don't be put off in making this call. Your insurance provider is likely to recommend that you also take out public liability insurance in case anyone who comes to visit suffers an injury in or around your home office. See the next page for a guide to all kinds of insurance.

Q: Do I need protection for when customers and contacts come to visit?

A: Yes, carry out a health and safety check, which is easy to do by following the steps set out by the Health and Safety Executive (**www.hse.gov.uk**) in their *Homeworking* guide (available at **bit.ly/aGDc8N**).

Q: Should I tell the neighbours?

A: Yes. When working from home, it's worth keeping your neighbours firmly on side. You don't want them getting annoyed by any deliveries or distractions. If you know of a time when there'll be an unusual amount of activity in your home office, let them know in advance and perhaps send a bottle of wine.

INSURANCE INS-AND-OUTS

There are different categories of insurance which you need to know about to secure the policy that's right for you. The main ones are:

1. **PROFESSIONAL INDEMNITY** – relevant to businesses offering services and knowledge. Provides protection if you receive a claim alleging a negligent act, error or omission committed by you in the course of the conduct of your professional business.

2. **PUBLIC LIABILITY** – advisable to have if clients are visiting your home office and/or you are supplying goods to consumers. This will protect you in the event of potential injury to business visitors and/or damages arising from the supply or sale of goods which have caused injury to a third party or their property.

3. **BUSINESS INTERRUPTION** – covers your potential loss of revenue following a material damage loss.

4. **EMPLOYER'S LIABILITY** – only applies when you have employees. Offers protection in the event of death or injury to them sustained in the course of their employment.

5. **MOTOR INSURANCE** – this is different to standard car insurance, which does not include business use. If you have a vehicle dedicated for business, you should buy motor insurance or get a business extension on your car insurance policy when using your existing car for business travel.

6. **HOME INSURANCE** – you are likely to already have a home insurance policy but this will generally not cover business activities carried out at home or business equipment within the home. Speak to your insurance provider and upgrade to a business policy. This is not usually costly but it will ensure you're protected.

Creating the perfect work environment

Wherever you've chosen to set up shop, create the perfect work environment by following this quick checklist to ensure you're working profitably and productively.

Find dedicated space

Try to create an area at home that functions as your dedicated workspace. That way you can better adjust into business mode. It's also useful for making clear to friends and family that when you're in your home office, you're working.

This dedicated space could be a spare room, in the attic, under the stairs, or even the garden shed.

Invest in a good desk and chair

You could be spending a good few hours each day at the desk and in your chair, so be sure they're both sturdy and comfortable. Buy a chair that's designed for computer use – and try it out first. The back experts say your feet should be flat on the floor and your back straight.

When it comes to computers, the top of your monitor or laptop screen should be at eye level and about an arm's length away from you. There are all sorts of docks that can help with this, but there's also no harm in using a sturdy pile of books and an external mouse/keyboard to achieve the same end.

Have a vision

Put a vision board up on the wall and stick pictures on it that represent your personal and business ambitions: places you want to visit, targets for the company, and people you enjoy spending time with. Glance at it each day. Remind yourself of everything you're working for.

Fit out your home office with furnishings from IKEA and sign up to the IKEA Business card to receive extra benefits. Visit **www.ikea.co.uk/business**

A SPRING CLEAN: Wondering what to do with all the stuff in the room that you want to use as your home office? Rent storage with a company like Bizspace (www.bizspace.co.uk) and have your goods accessible but out of the way, or give them to a recycling company so that your unwanted items can go to a home that does want them!

Roam free

Install Wi-Fi so it's possible to work from anywhere on the property. To get started you need a wireless router. You may have received one free from your internet service provider. If not, check out respectable suppliers such as Netgear (**www.netgear.co.uk**). See 'Getting connected' on page 46 if you need support.

PETS AND PLANTS: Having plants in your home office can reduce work-stress, experts say. Seeing a growth in greenery can also help you feel less alone, and it helps with humidity levels, dust and productivity. Likewise, pets are known to reduce stress and can be an excellent source of company!

Support on tap

And finally, surround yourself with supporters. Friends or family, peers in online forums, contacts met at events; they can all help when it comes to celebrating your success or raising your spirits on a day that doesn't quite go as planned.

On pages 158 we cover where to go to find support and access mentors. For Oliver Sidwell, support was close to home when he started his business, RateMyPlacement:

"When we launched RateMyPlacement, my two co-founders and I worked from separate home offices. Mine happened to be my old bedroom back in the family home. I graduated from Loughborough University where the business had started, moved back in with my folks and the business of building the company started from there.

"As my dad also ran his business from home we often met in the kitchen at lunchtime and I shared progress from the day. Dad offered advice and guidance which, in the early stages, proved invaluable. I'm now living in London and the company is 20 people strong but I still hark back to those early days of sage advice, mum's welcome cups of tea and a top-notch laundry service!"

Leaving home

If an external office is right for you from the start, visit sites such as **www.startupbritain.co/spaces** to find available space in enterprise hubs, co-working spaces, government buildings and serviced offices. All needs and budgets catered for! See page 161 for details on 'accelerators', that come complete with space as part of the package.

IN THE KIT

Get one month's free virtual office or one month free in any Bizspace unit.

Get a value business start-up package from Regus, including impressive business address, call answering, mail-handling, business mentoring, drop-in business lounges and more.

Get 'Three Days, One Club' Membership at Kennington Park, Enterprise House or Barley Mow reduced to £150+VAT pcm for the first three months from Club Workspace.

Alain Desmier and Mike Laming decided Club Workspace would be their preferred space to house the expansion of their app business . . .

CASE STUDY

NAME: Alain Desmier | BUSINESS: OrSaveIt

Alain Desmier is confident that he and business partner Mike Laming have found a niche in the impulse saving market. The co-founders of OrSaveIt are building technology to support anyone who wants to put money aside each month towards a saving goal but doesn't want to go through the hassle of opening a new bank account.

"We started the business in July 2012. Mike and I looked at our personal spending and realised the £2 cup of coffee we bought each day (sometimes twice a day) didn't seem like much by itself, but really added up over time. We realised we were spending hundred of pounds on these types of impulse buys." Alain and Mike wanted to build an app that would help them and others turn those impulse buys into steady and painless savings.

"OrSaveIt allows users to make impulse saves from their phone and build them towards a savings goal. If you decide to forgo your morning cappuccino, for instance, the OrSaveIt app allows you to deduct £2.50 from your current account into your OrSaveIt goal fund. OrSaveIt helps our users to change their spending and saving behaviour by asking them commit to savings targets and allowing them to capture every day sacrifices to meet those targets."

There are similar start-ups in the US that are in the impulse savings space but they all require you to have a specific bank account. We wanted to build something that was open to everyone, regardless of who you banked with."

Alain was invited to speak at an event hosted at Club Workspace and was immediately taken by the atmosphere and flexibility of the space. "It was the first place I turned to when I went looking for an office."

Alain and Mike support each other and contribute different talents to the business; their backgrounds are in commercial and technology sectors. Support has also been on hand from Club Workspace members who are at the same stage of start-up development. As well as peer support, Club Workspace puts on regular events for members and non-members with experts speaking on topics from law to mentoring.

The beta version of their app launches in January 2013 with a full launch in April. The team will be well housed throughout!

- **orsaveit.com** | @orsaveit

7. YOUR TECH SETUP

P utting together a tech setup for your new business needn't mean starting from scratch or spending lots of money. Once your business starts to grow, you can upgrade your tech as and when money becomes available.

To start with, there are affordable and free solutions that can get you up and running in no time at all. Chances are, you have some of them already.

So, let's take a look at what you might already have and what you might need to buy. We'll separate them by hardware and software.

Hardware

Computer

When starting out, using a shared computer will be just fine. Bear in mind, however, that in the first few months of starting your business, you may find yourself working more hours than usual trying to put it all together. So let your friends and family know you may be hogging the computer!

Also, when your business starts to grow, the information you collect – info on your customers, clients and contacts; including financial details – will become more and more valuable. You might then start to think twice about sharing your computer with other people.

You may already have your own laptop. If you don't, when you've got a bit of money behind you, look into buying one for your new business. Budget laptops start at around £300, but when buying a computer it sometimes pays to buy the best you can afford in order to prepare for the future.

Processor

The processor is the speed of your computer. The higher the number, the faster your computer can run.

Memory

More memory (RAM) improves performance and enables your computer to run more programs at once. A common frustration amongst computer users is how long it can take to launch programs and switch between them. More RAM equals less waiting.

Hard drive

The hard drive gives you space for data and programs. This can easily be expanded with an additional, external, hard drive. You may be surprised at how quickly it will fill up, if your laptop is your only computer and you're also storing personal data, like music and photos, on it.

Peripherals

Multifunction printer

Even though I find myself using it less these days, I still think it's too early to pronounce the printer dead, especially if you use a multifunction printer like I do.

It's a real space-saver – imagine keeping a printer, scanner, photocopier and fax machine in one office. Mine sits neatly on my desk and is handy when I want to email sketches to my designer. He uses his to archive printed documents. When he receives important letters, for example, he scans them into his computer and recycles the hard copy! We're both on our way to paperless home offices.

External hard drive

External hard drives are great for adding more storage capacity to your computer but they're especially useful for backing up your machine. This is an important process, which you should do regularly – imagine what would happen if your computer crashed and wouldn't restart, or if it was dropped or stolen.

Macs have backing-up software built-in; as do the latest PCs. If not, try SuperDuper! for the Mac and True Image for the PC.

- SuperDuper! | **www.shirt-pocket.com/SuperDuper**
- True Image | **www.acronis.com**

Keyboard and mouse

If you're going to use a laptop, you probably won't get an additional keyboard and mouse. But you should think about it. Lots of time hunched over your laptop screen is no good for your neck and back. With an additional keyboard and mouse, and a stand that raises your laptop to eye-level, you can prevent a lifetime of aches and pains.

Some companies produce keyboards/mice which are ergonomically designed to prevent repetitive strain injury (RSI).

VoIP phones

You can make serious savings on your phone bill by using a VoIP phone. VoIP stands for 'voice over internet protocol' and basically means making calls over the internet rather than your phone line. As such, it's a much cheaper way of making calls (it's sometimes free). And it's the easiest way to set up a second line. The VoIP phone I use is made by a company called IPEVO.

- IPEVO | **www.ipevo.com**

Software

You may already be using many of these programs, so there's no need to splash out when setting up your business. Once it grows you can upgrade to more advanced versions if required. To start, here are the basics. Later we'll look at software (much of it free or very affordable) for when your business is up and running.

Office software

The industry standard in office software is Microsoft Office. If you're trying to save money, try these free alternatives:

- OpenOffice.org | www.openoffice.org
- Google Docs | www.google.com/docs

Both do pretty much everything that Microsoft Office does, and can open and save Microsoft Office files as well.

Web browser

Internet Explorer and Safari both do a good job when it comes to web browsing, as does Firefox. But there's a browser I use that I think is better. It's called Google Chrome and it's faster, more secure and more customisable.

You can add features that will help you do your work and manage your lifestyle. These include features to control your music (without having to switch programs), comparison shop and even change the way your browser looks. It's a free, small download, and it works on Macs and PCs. Its speedy and uncluttered nature makes it particularly good for netbook use.

- Google Chrome | www.google.com/chrome

Email

If you've got Microsoft Office you might use Outlook (or Entourage, as it's called in the Mac version), which is Outlook Express's big sister. It includes calendar and address book features, but it's not free (or cheap). On Macs, Mail is standard.

An alternative is provided by the people who make the Firefox browser. It's called Thunderbird and can do pretty much everything that Outlook can. You can also use it with web-based mail, like Gmail.

- Thunderbird | www.getthunderbird.com

Instant messaging and VoIP

Lots of instant messaging programs also allow you to make video and voice calls. Skype integrates text, voice and video chat. With it you can make free calls to other Skype users and to landline or mobile phones for a small fee, deducted from pay-as-you-go style Skype credit.

You can assign a landline-esque phone number to your Skype account in order to receive calls at your computer, using a VoIP handset, or divert calls to your mobile when out and about.

• Skype | **www.skype.com**

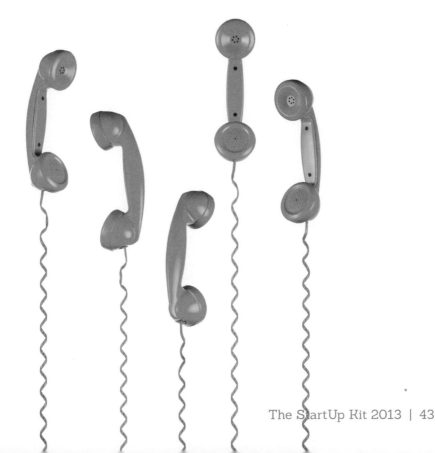

Support

If you're in need of assistance with anything from hardware set-up to software installation, call in the help of a local IT expert. You may know a neighbour who's a dab hand at technology. If not, check out one of a growing number of companies who send a 'geek' direct to your door.

- Geeks-on-Wheels | www.geeks-on-wheels.com
- KnowHow | www.knowhow.com
- Geek Squad | www.geeksquad.co.uk

On the move

Now that you've found the right technology for your office it's time to take it outside. If you ever get tired of your four walls, it's good to know that it's possible to work elsewhere. With a few simple tips and tricks you can enjoy total flexibility, and work from almost anywhere.

With your computer

If you have a laptop, you pretty much have all you need to work on the move. Almost all laptops come with built-in wireless receivers, so you can hop onto Wi-Fi in public places like coffee shops and libraries. But if you're not sure whether there'll be ample power supply where you're going, a spare battery is well worth considering.

SHOULD I BUY A TABLET COMPUTER OR A LAPTOP?

Like the rest of the world, you've probably been tempted by gorgeous tablet computers like Apple's iPad. But should you buy one instead of a laptop? Can you really get as much business-work done on a tablet?

Well, it really depends on the nature of your business. If you'll be out and about a lot, visiting clients and customers, then buying a tablet becomes a serious consideration. But if your work will involve lots of sitting at a desk or writing long documents, you may find that a tablet PC is not for you. The iPad is constantly improving as a business machine thanks to the App Store, but it still needs an external keyboard to cope with long writing sessions.

The future of computing could lie somewhere between tablets and laptops: ultrabooks. Ultrabooks are really thin, fast laptops. They have traditional features, like a full-size keyboard and trackpad, but usually no DVD drive and limited hard drive storage. That's okay, though, as a lot of your work will take place in the 'Cloud' (more on that later!). Because of their size and weight, ultrabooks are really portable.

Getting connected

You'll need broadband right from the start: during your research, while you're setting up your business, through to when it grows and takes over the world!

Your two main options are ADSL broadband, which is offered by companies like BT, Orange and Sky, and cable broadband from Virgin Media. The biggest difference is that ADSL requires a phone line, while cable broadband does not.

The advantage of cable broadband is that if you don't have a landline phone, and always use your mobile, you can save money by not having to pay line rental on your phone as well as on your internet connection. It's often faster, too, but you'll need to check whether it's available in your area. ADSL broadband is more commonplace and there are lots of companies offering it. As always, read the fine print before you sign anything. Here are some things to look out for:

Price

Some broadband prices seem really cheap but often the prices advertised are for the first few months of an 18-month contract, so make sure you know what you're getting into.

Usage

Some broadband companies will set restrictions on the amount of data you can download in a month and sometimes even charge you extra if you go over your agreed limit. These limits rarely affect most users, but if your business is the kind that needs to send and receive lots of information, look for deals with generous monthly download allowances. Or, better still, unlimited downloads.

Customer support

If you're installing broadband for the first time, you might need some help setting up and, once you're up and running, for what to do when your connection suddenly drops. For these sorts of queries it's handy to have good customer support, so check to see what's on offer and, crucially, how much it should cost to call for help.

Network

Setting up a network used to be the work of professionals and, I suppose, in big companies it still is. But setting one up for your home by yourself is much easier these days.

There are two types of wireless router: one for ADSL internet service providers, like Sky and BT, and another for cable internet, like Virgin Media. Check with your internet service provider to find out which is the best router for your type of connection.

If you didn't get a router from your provider, check out Netgear.

- Netgear | **www.netgear.co.uk**

The Cloud

If you already use web mail, you'll be accustomed to the idea of your messages and contacts being available from any computer or device connected to the internet. So, how about running your entire business from any computer or device anywhere?

The Cloud refers to web apps. You run them through your web browser and all the data is stored online, so in effect you can use them from pretty much any computer anywhere!

The best example is provided by Google, whose Google Apps (**www.google.com/a**) offering includes email, instant messaging, a calendar, word processor, spreadsheet and presentation software, as well as a website builder. It's free and easy to use.

All the work you do is stored in 'The Cloud' so you can log in and out from anywhere and see the same information. Also, if your computer crashes or you buy a new system you won't lose any data or have to reinstall it on a new machine.

TEN FREE CLOUD APPS FOR YOUR BUSINESS

Cloud apps are not only fantastically useful, they don't take up room on your computer and you don't have to worry about backing up your data. They're also, more often than not, free to use.

Here are ten of our favourite free cloud apps for business.

1. Dropbox (**www.dropbox.com**) | Dropbox is like a thumb drive in the sky. It's a folder that sits on your computer, but its contents are stored remotely and synced across other computers and devices that are signed into your Dropbox account. No-nonsense sharing, if you're working with others, and peace of mind that all your work is backed up.

2. Evernote (**www.evernote.com**) | Evernote is a bit like Dropbox, but for your brain. It helps you "remember everything" by allowing you to capture notes and ideas, photos and screen grabs, sounds and links, sync them automatically to the cloud and access them from practically anywhere – great for the planning stages of your business.

3. Google Docs (**docs.google.com**) | As broadband gets quicker and more reliable, Google Docs is becoming a bit of a threat to Microsoft Office. It includes apps for word processing, spreadsheets, presentations, drawings and forms – except all the apps run inside your browser rather than on your desktop. All of your work is stored in the cloud and it's super easy to collaborate with others in real time on the same document.

4. Gmail and Google Calendar (**mail.google.com**, **calendar.google.com**) | I've mentioned Gmail before, but did you know Google also make excellent calendar software? Both are really useful if you plan to work on the move.

5. Google Analytics (**www.google.com/analytics**) | When your website is up and running, you'll want to know how many people are visiting. Google Analytics, like most of Google's services, is free, and helps you understand your website statistics, including where your visitors are from, which pages

they visited the most, and how they found your website in the first place.

6. HootSuite (**www.hootsuite.com**) | If social media is part of your marketing plan – and it probably is! – there's no better way to manage your social media presence than with HootSuite. It keeps you on top of your Twitter, Facebook and LinkedIn accounts, as well as what your customers and potential customers are saying about your business.

7. Delicious (**www.delicious.com**) | Delicious is a bookmarking service that keeps all of your important links in the cloud so you can get to them from any computer.

8. Toodledo (**www.toodledo.com**) | There's so much to do when starting a business, but you can keep on top of all your tasks with this free app. Get tasks out of your inbox by forwarding them to your Toodledo email address, organise them by folders, tags, context and subtasks, and sync them with your smartphone.

9. Basecamp (**www.basecamp.com**) | If some tasks involve other people and form part of larger projects, check out project management software, Basecamp. It allows you to share files, deliver projects on time and keep communication organised and out of your inbox.

10. MailChimp (**www.mailchimp.com**) | To make sure your business message is in other people's inboxes, put together a newsletter with MailChimp, send it out to your customer mailing list and track its success. Just make sure people have signed up to your mailing list before hitting 'send'!

8. WORKING 5 TO 9

You don't need to give up your studies or throw in the day job to get all this done. Nor do you need to for the next two stages – launch and growth. You can plan the business, register the business and continue to run the business successfully by 'working 5 to 9' – this is the term I apply to the five-million-plus people in the UK who are working or studying by day and building a business at night and weekends.

It's a sensible way to start and grow. If you're working a day job, you give yourself the time to build confidence and cash flow in the business, and can keep putting money aside until you're ready to go full time in your own venture.

Here's what you need to do regarding your current job and boss in order to make this as smooth as possible.

The contract

If you have written terms and conditions of employment they are likely to contain reference to the pursuit of personal business ventures outside your contracted working hours. The clauses to look out for include 'the employee's duties and obligations' and what is commonly known as 'whole time and effort'. These clauses require the employee to devote the whole of their time, attention and abilities to the business of the employer.

If your contract contains these or similar clauses, don't despair, as it doesn't necessarily mean you can't pursue your business. Many employment contracts are drafted using standard templates with little consideration to personal circumstance. You know your job better than anyone, so if you don't think your business venture will affect the way you do your

job, it probably won't – and your employer will recognise this. Having checked how things stand in the contract, it's time to talk things through with your boss.

The conversation

Treat it as an amicable and informal conversation to gauge your employer's initial reaction.

I asked Patrick Lockton, a qualified lawyer, for his take on the matter and advice on how employees should go about having this conversation:

"When you approach your employer, be prepared to negotiate, be flexible and compromise. If you think it appropriate, make it clear your business venture will in no shape or form affect your ability to do your job or affect your employer's interests. If anything, it will make you a better, more confident and experienced employee and it will not cost your employer a thing."

Patrick goes on to say:

"After having such a conversation, you can do one of two things:

1. if your employer has not expressed any concerns about your intentions and you have no concerns of your own, disclose your intentions to your employer anyway. Treat it as something you want to do for the sake of clarity and for the record, as opposed to something you want their permission for; or

2. if your employer has expressed concerns, try and negotiate a package that you are both happy with. Address their concerns, agree some ground rules and get their permission in writing. Give your employer as much helpful information as possible. If you are going to need some time off or to change your hours then this is the time to bring it up.

"Always take written notes so that you don't forget what was said and so you can remind your employer what was agreed."

So long as you're not competing with your employer or breaching their trust, you shouldn't have any problem at all in pursuing your 5 to 9 ambitions. After all, as Patrick says, your employer benefits from all the new skills you're picking up, and it doesn't cost them a penny in training or resources!

Richard Baldock knows all about working 5 to 9. It's worked out well for him as his employer became a customer . . .

CASE STUDY

Richard Baldock started his company, Desktag, in 2008 when he first came up with the idea for slick-looking self-assembly name-tags for desks. But with a busy home life and young family, turning the idea into reality and getting products manufactured only happened in early 2012.

Richard's product is a sturdy, freestanding plastic sleeve that can sit on everything from a hotel helpdesk to a speaker's lectern. You fill it with a stylish paper tag designed with the help of the company's creator app. Just print it off when you're happy, fold twice, and slide it in place. It's much better than hastily scrawled paper notes, and more flexible and afforable than engraved metal or laminated plastic.

It was whilst at work that Richard spotted the potential for the product. "I've always worked in big open plan offices," he says. "Finding people in that kind of place can be a problem. How often have you walked through an office searching for someone, feeling embarrassed to be staring at rows of people and screens, and not knowing who to turn to? With ever-changing technology and office churn, along with flexible working styles like 'hot-desking', the need to identify the whereabouts of staff, contractors and visitors has become a challenge for any organisation. I thought Desktag could be the answer."

Richard developed the business while holding down his day job. "My employer is aware of my business; I made the decision early on that it was important that they knew. I was a director of the company and planning to use social media networks in the evenings to build my brand. When telling my employer I planned what I was going to say. I actually turned it into a mini pitch, selling the benefits of the product and how it could help carefully our organisation.

"Once my idea was discussed it was clear there was no conflict of interest so they were comfortable with me pursuing in my own time. To aid my presentation I created a branded tag for the HR director and she liked it so much she placed an order. So my employer become my first customer!"

When it comes to time management, Richard is disciplined and doesn't let desktag interfere with the 9–5 job. He embraces technology to catch up on email and social media links in the evening.

"I've recently moved my domain to Google Apps for Business, and my core files to Dropbox, which means I can access all data from anywhere. If I have anything of any interest to say to my Twitter followers, I use Buffer (bufferapp.com) to schedule them; it means I have a varied spread of times when I tweet."

Throughout 2012 Richard has concentrated on building the Desktag product portfolio and ensuring both brand and product are protected through intellectual property protection. The software development skills required for the business have been sourced via Elance.com.

With the product-set ready, the focus for 2013 is on promotion and building the brand.

"The limited amount of promotion I have done is mainly via networking events and social media channels; you can meet some fantastic contacts through these and gain valuable feedback. I have a bag full of tags with me at all times to display at events and I take along a battery powered printer so I can create and print tags live at events. The tag creation process is really easy – it just uses a piece of A4 paper."

With promotion at the ready, expect to see great things from this start-up over the next 12 months. Tag that!

- www.desktag.com | @desktag

9. STARTING ON A BUDGET AND STRAIGHTFORWARD FINANCE

It has never been more straightforward to build a business on a shoestring of a budget and keep on top of finances with basic spreadsheets or software. You probably already have a computer and a mobile phone, so you might not need to buy much more equipment (depending on your business). Here are some tips for keeping costs low.

Start the business from home

Why take on the cost of an office when the spare room/attic/garden shed will do just as well? Think of the money you'll save: no premises, no commute, no overpriced sandwiches at lunchtime . . . !

Embrace social media

Make the most of free or low-cost technology tools to raise your profile and make sales. Chapter 12 offers details of the major social media tools and how they can best be used to your benefit.

Beg, borrow and barter!

When starting out, access all the free and discounted resources you can.

THE BEAUTY OF BARTER: Many start-up businesses barter their goods and services, e.g. "I'll produce a sales brochure for you, in exchange for a handmade cushion for my living room." This works well – both parties get what they want. But take heed of the tax implications. Bartering means money doesn't show up in your accounts, but there has been an exchange of goods and services which implies a taxable activity. The taxman could view bartering as a way to avoid tax. Nevertheless, with so many beneficial arrangements underway, maybe it's time they revised the tax situation?

Access deals

The StartUp Kit comes complete with tons of deals and offers from leading brands. You can view all of them at the back of the book and activate them online at www.enterprisenation.com/startupkit2013. Source other deals on the StartUp Britain marketplace (www.startupbritain.co) or daily deals site Huddlebuy (www.huddlebuy.com).

Neil Brewster has benefited from the art of bartering to secure prime office space . . .

CASE STUDY

NAME: **Neil Brewster** | BUSINESS: **Lightning Apps**

After a 20-year career in the freight-forwarding industry that involved stints living in the USA and Asia, Neil Brewster returned to the UK disillusioned with employment and decided to start his own business in January 2012.

The company is a digital agency that designs and develops apps – hence its name – and when it came to making his first sales, Neil decided to stick to the industry he knew.

"To secure our first client I approached the largest logistics event at The NEC and offered to build an app in return for a free exhibition stand. I used the logistics industry as an initial target point as I had credibility and a good reputation in this area and knew that app technology wasn't being adopted by the people exhibiting and attending. I then used the whole three days selling my heart out to everybody there."

Neil promotes the business in a host of ways, including regular speaking appearances at local business breakfasts and lunch events on the topic of technology and social media in business. He also again built a free app, this time for his local chamber of commerce, in exchange for marketing to their members.

"I use social media as well as Google AdWords, LinkedIn Ads, press releases and PR methods to gain leads. I network tirelessly and attend as many events as I possibly can. I actively sell myself and do a lot of research, targeting clients who I think will need me. I pick the phone up and speak to them."

This activity has paid off. The company recently celebrated its win in the Innovation and Technology category of the Richmond Business Awards. On the night, Neil picked up six new potential clients and has been contacted by others since.

The App Store on Apple's iOS devices accounts for around 40% of revenue.

"The approval process in Google Play for an Android app takes around one hour. For iTunes, the approval process has been taking on average six working days although you can experience approval times of up to three weeks. The trick with gaining quick approval is to keep the code clean and as minimal as possible. Once uploaded Apple notify you and keep you up to date with where you are in the approval process and email you with a download link when they are about to put it live."

When it comes to the space in which this development happens, Neil put his bartering skills to work.

"I started by renting desk space in hub-working places (which was also great for networking) and progressed to my own office in Richmond by doing a deal with a client. When visiting their office I noticed they had an office tucked away which was not being used. It looked perfect for about six people and would help with my expansion plans. They had many apps that needed building so we agreed on a contra deal: a number of free development days per month in return for the space."

Neil's wife may soon be joining this growing company as she is currently studying Computer Science as a mature student and is keen to be involved in the business on graduation. There's much to be done: 2013 sees see a relaunch of the website and a competition for 16–18 year olds to devise the 'best app idea', with two winners receiving an apprenticeship with Lightning Apps and the opportunity to develop their ideas.

So not only is Neil realising his own entrepreneurial vision – he's helping the next generation do the same!

- **www.lightningapps.com** | @lightning_apps

These tips and techniques will help your budgeting, but if you think you'll need more funding, here are a few places to look.

Funding

Friends and family

Friends and family are people you can trust – and asking them for money hopefully won't come with strings attached. Do consider having a written agreement, though, that covers the amount borrowed and a payback schedule.

Start-Up Loans

Aged between 18 and 24 and starting a business? You'll like the sound of Start-Up Loans then! These are loans of up to £2,500 made to young entrepreneurs across the UK. Alongside a loan, you also receive a mentor who offers help throughout your business journey.

- www.startuploans.co.uk

Elena Mingas applied for and received a start-up loan which has given her new start-up the breathing space required to trade . . .

CASE STUDY

NAME: **Elena Mingas** | BUSINESS: **Tangle Dress Design**

After graduating from the University of Central Lancashire in 2011 with a first class honours degree in fashion design, Elena Mingas immediately landed a job in Dubai for a luxury boutique where she headed styling, visual merchandising and buying. It was also the place from where she started to sell her own dress designs – something that soon led to her own business.

"I returned to the UK in March 2012 to pursue my dream of having my own business and I've been working on it ever since. As fabulous as Dubai is, the job wasn't for me and I wasn't learning anything, so I felt the time was right to head home with experience under my belt and make a go of it. I started the business in September 2012."

Elena's mum was also keeping an eye out for opportunities for her daughter's new business and saw a feature on the government-backed start-up loans scheme in *The*

Sun. Seeing they had been launched to help young people become their own boss, Elena liked the Start-Up Loans company on Facebook to stay updated on when she'd be able to apply.

"When it was time to apply, I did so via Facebook and received confirmation of my application. Then I was contacted by John Cannon, a loan manager for Business Finance Solutions in Manchester, who invited me to come for a chat and talk through my business plan and cash flow forecast. John basically wanted to see that I was serious and had a viable business plan. The meeting went really well and I was contacted a couple of days later to say the loan was approved subject to a credit check. Within a couple of weeks from meeting John, I had the loan in my bank and my business was underway. It was a really positive experience."

Business Finance Solutions acts as the distribution partner for Start-Up Loans in Manchester, and there are similar organisations working with the scheme across the country. They can assist applicants at all stages – if you apply for a loan without a business plan and cash flow forecast, you receive introductions to people who can help.

"The whole process is hassle free," says Elena. "Really all you need is an idea and a hunger for success."

As well as receiving up to £2,500 in funding, successful applicants to Start-Up Loans are matched with a mentor. In Elena's case, her mentor is a local entrepreneur, Carl Smith.

"Carl has been a great help to me and invaluable for those things you just need to sense-check with someone. I personally think a mentor is more important than the money because if you're determined enough you will find the cash but you won't necessarily find someone willing to give up their time to advise you and who shares your vision for the business."

With the loan in her account, a new shop opened and mentor onboard, Elena plans to build her client base. "Eventually I aim to make Tangle Dress Design the go-to place for bespoke evening wear and have other retails outlets around the country." When she achieves it, this young entrepreneur will thank the Start-Up Loans Company for giving her the means to get going.

- **www.tangledressdesign.com** | **www.facebook.com/TangleDressDesign** | **@TangleDresses**

Crowd funding

Crowd funding is fast becoming a popular route to secure start-up and follow-on funding. It involves sourcing funds from a crowd of others. Check out the following links for sites that offer this service.

- CrowdCube | www.crowdcube.com

- Kickstarter | www.kickstarter.com

- Seedrs | www.seedrs.com

- PleaseFund.Us | www.pleasefund.us
  (with a focus on creative projects)

- IWOCA | www.iwoca.co.uk (for online
  retailers only and for working capital as
  opposed to start-up funding)

The bank

Ask to speak to a small business advisor at your local bank. Take a copy of your business plan with you and be prepared to talk it through.

A CLEAR DIVISION: Open a bank account early on so you don't mix up your business and personal finances, which may complicate record keeping.

Shelling out the funds

Apply to the Shell LiveWIRE Grand Ideas Awards to be in with a chance of winning £1,000. Four awards are made each month to anyone aged 16 to 30 who is starting a business in the UK or within their first 12 months of trading.

- www.shell-livewire.org/awards

See page 120 for more details on Shell LiveWIRE and other awards to enter.

Investors

Angel investors and venture capitalists can help raise large amounts of start-up funding or development capital for businesses looking to grow. It might be an idea to consider this route further down the line. It doesn't have to be a gruesome experience (à la *Dragons' Den*), though, as there are plenty of funds and investors out there who are eager to part with their money and back good ideas. What's more, the government has made it financially attractive for angels to invest through the Seed Enterprise Investment Scheme which offers individual income tax relief of 50% and exemption from capital gains tax (CGT) on any proceeds of sale of a SEIS investment.

Visit the dedicated SEIS website (www.seis.co.uk) for details and the Business Finance For You site (www.businessfinanceforyou.co.uk), which offers a listing of available grants and funds, searchable by your local area.

In the words of an Angel

Andy Yates is an experienced angel investor and serial entrepreneur. In terms of what he looks for, he says:

"Great businesses are created by great people. I always look out for the three Ps – passion, personality and perseverance. I also back entrepreneurs who really listen and learn. The ability to be flexible, take on board advice and feedback and adapt a product or service to win customers is the real key to unlocking success."

- Angels Den | www.angelsden.co.uk
- Funding Circle | www.fundingcircle.com
- Find Invest Grow | www.findinvestgrow.com
- Springboard | www.springboard.com
- UK Business Angels Association | www.bbaa.org.uk

See page 161 for details on accelerator programmes that will take your business from start to growth at speed, and often come attached with funding.

Straightforward finance

When planning a business you'll want to be sure earnings are higher than outgoings. Earnings are also referred to as revenue, turnover or income and this should be a greater figure than outgoings, overheads or costs. Let's look at the items that come within each category.

Incoming

Earn from selling your product or service and any associated income opportunities. For example, you set up a business selling unique handmade cushions. From the outset, earn income from:

- Selling 24 x handmade cushions at £25 per cushion = £600 income per week
- Speaking at events to teach others how to make cushions = £150 per event
- Custom requests, e.g. a unique and one-off production = £75 per item
- Developing a blog on the topic of cushions that attracts cushion-istas as readers and paying advertisers as your customers – £priceless!

Outgoings

Here are the costs; some payable at start-up stage and others ongoing:

- **Salary** – how much do you need to pay yourself? (You will be pleasantly surprised at how thriftily you can live when not commuting.)
- **Property** – start the business from home and avoid the cost of a pricey office.
- **Raw materials and equipment** – what are the materials you need to deliver and promote your finished cushions? And do you need any equipment to make that product; a sewing machine, computer, printer, smartphone or camera?
- **Insurance** – be insured from the start and choose a policy that covers all your needs.
- **Website/promotion materials** – we will cover in Chapters 10–12 how you can build a home on the web and promote the business on a shoestring of a budget.

Keep records of 'Incoming' and 'Outgoing' in a basic Excel spreadsheet as in the following. See page 156 for an example invoice and how to keep a record of invoices raised and amounts paid.

INCOMING	
Product sales	£xx
Sponsorship/Advertising	£xx
Other contracts	£xx
OUTGOINGS	
Salary	(£xx)
IT	(£xx)
Office	(£xx)
Raw materials/equipment	(£xx)
Insurance	(£xx)
Marketing & promotion	(£xx)
Other	(£xx)
PROFIT	**£XX**

II. LAUNCH

You have your idea. It's supported by research and a plan pointing you in the right direction. You've sorted out all the technology you need to get going. And with the company registered, it's time to get into business by making sales and some noise.

66 Be a sponge: absorb as much help and support as you can! Approach others. Listen. Join a networking group. All too often I see entrepreneurs over-protective of their venture. They miss vital guidance. **99**

– Claire Young, founder, School Speakers

10. CREATE A FIRST IMPRESSION

You may have started out by making sales to friends and family who know and trust you to deliver. To attract new customers, it's important to create the right first impression, whether that customer meets you at an event or visits your home on the web. Here's guidance to getting it right and offering a professional welcome.

Your home on the web

You have the tools and connection to get online. The first thing to do is build a presence through a blog, website or store. Not only is a website your window to the world and home on the web, it has become an essential requirement for any new business. Your site can be used as a powerful marketing tool and a way to make money. Having the right technology and knowledge allows you to build, develop and maintain your site. And you can do it all in-house.

Let's look at the three main ways to develop a professional-looking online presence.

1. Blogging

Blogging is a website or part of a website that's regularly updated by an individual or a group of bloggers. There are blogs on any number of topics and the fact that anyone can start blogging for free makes the medium diverse and exciting.

It's an easy way to get online, as you write posts on your topic of choice, upload images and video, and become the go-to place for customers looking for your advice/tips/services/products. Search engines love blogs and the more you write, the higher up the search-engine ranks you will go. Writing regularly is likely to lead to a loyal readership and it's an effective way to communicate your news with existing and potential customers. Readers can add their comments to your entries if you allow them, and you can use your blog to answer questions and establish yourself as an expert in your field.

IT'S FREE AND EASY to get blogging:

- Blogger | www.blogger.com
- Typepad | www.typepad.com
- WordPress | www.wordpress.com

See Chapter 11 for details on how to make money from your blog.

Now you see me

After getting to grips with blogging, why not try your hand at vlogging? This stands for video blogging and is an effective way to interact with customers who want to see you, your products and other happy customers. Vlogging expert, Niamh Guckian, offers tips on how to vlog like a pro:

VLOG HOW-TO

"Vlogging can help you tell people your story: a demonstration of your skills, an atmosphere piece, or an interview.

THE GEAR: "Become an expert on your chosen camera, whether a phone or something fancier.

"Where possible use manual control with your camera – this applies to white balance, exposure and focus. Learn the rules and *then* have fun breaking them.

"Use focus and depth of field to add style to your shooting. Using a tripod sets your work apart from amateur shooting and allows for good steady shot composition.

SAFETY: "Using a small camera can make you feel like you can take risks that you wouldn't otherwise. This has advantages at times but don't take unnecessary risks. Don't shoot from rooftops or get into water!

LIGHT: "As a video-blogger, you will mostly be working with available or natural light. Try to get the most from what's available at the time.

SOUND: "Audio recording is a specialist art form. What we need to achieve as self-shooters is clean and non-distorted sound. Distorted audio is not fixable, and can usually be prevented.

INTERVIEWS: "If your piece is interview-based, engage with the contributor, communicate with them and let them know clearly what you want them to do. Create an atmosphere where the contributor is comfortable, and make sure they know they can stop and start again, or ask questions.

"Make sure the interview is a sequence, that it has a beginning, middle and end, and can stand alone if necessary.

EXPORT AND UPLOAD: "Learn about the optimum settings and platforms for your finished piece."

2. Your own website

Build your own website that you can spec to your own requirements or invest in a template website. Let's look at both options.

DIY

You have decided to build your own site or have a developer take care of it for you.

The first thing to do is buy a domain. A domain makes up a part of your website and email address. So, for example, the domain name I own is enterprisenation.com. My website address is **www.enterprisenation.com** and my email address is **emma@enterprisenation.com**. Both use the enterprisenation.com domain name.

A domain isn't only your address on the web, it's also a big part of your brand, so think carefully when choosing one. There are domain registration companies whose websites allow you to check for available domain names and often suggest available alternatives.

Registering a domain name doesn't give you a website, just an address for it (and an email address). Think of it like reserving a car parking space. You've got the space, now you need to buy the car!

A hosting company will sort you out with the web space to host your site. This is measured in megabytes and gigabytes, just like the information on your computer.

In terms of how much web space you will need, basic hosting packages offer about 250 MB of space, but anything over 1 or 2 GB is more sensible and will also allow you to handle more traffic as your website grows more popular.

With a domain name and web space, potential customers should be able to type your website address into their browser and find out all about your business – just as soon as you've built your site. Finding a hosting company shouldn't be hard. Most domain registration companies, including those mentioned above, offer web space as a package; and hosting companies usually offer domain registration, too.

When it comes to hiring a designer, have a think about what you'd like your website to do for your business. The easiest way to start is to think of your website as a brochure, but remember to include the following pages at the very least.

1&1 Internet Ltd
www.1and1.co.uk

123-reg
www.123-reg.co.uk

Easily Ltd
www.easily.co.uk

Choose a designer who has carried out work you like the look of and for companies in a similar kind of sector to your own. That way, the designer will understand what site you're after – and what your kind of visitor will be looking for, as well as how they like to browse and buy.

BRIEF A WEB DESIGNER/DEVELOPER

Here's Emily Hewett's (**www.birdsontheblog.co.uk**) advice on how best to brief a web designer/developer:

"WHO ARE YOU? Give a short summary of who you are and what you do. This will help the designer tune in to your particular sector. You'll also need to tell them about your market and how you fit into the larger scheme of things – e.g. competitors, local and national.

"WHAT DO YOU WANT TO ACHIEVE? For example: data capture, sales generation, footfall increase, etc.?

"WHO ARE YOU TALKING TO? Outline a profile of your customer. Who are you targeting? Break it down in terms of sex, age, average income and location.

"WHAT TONE ARE YOU USING? Deciding on how you speak to your audience is important. You may be writing the copy yourself or you may have a copywriter to do this for you. In this section of the brief tell the designer if it's a laid-back chatty tone or formal. The tone of the copy needs to be reflected in the design.

"WHAT ARE YOUR LIKES AND DISLIKES? Provide examples wherever possible. It might be a certain colour palette or illustration style or it could be a format. Any of these things help the designer understand what you're looking for.

"ARE THERE ANY MANDATORY ELEMENTS? Fonts, colours, logos, legal text, images, etc. This way they can make sure they produce something on-brand, adhering to your corporate image.

"WHAT'S YOUR BUDGET? A good designer won't take a large budget and fit a job to it. They should find the most cost-effective way of producing exactly what you want. But if you have a small budget, the designer will have to make decisions based on that.

"WHEN DO YOU WANT IT? Make sure the deadline is clear.

"HAVE YOU COVERED EVERYTHING? Show the brief to a colleague or friend to see if they understand it. Once happy, send or talk it through with your designer and invite questions so they are aware you are approachable and that you are both working from the same list of requirements.

Template site

If DIY feels and sounds too much like hard work, there are a number of companies offering template websites that come with domain registration, hosting, e-commerce and a basic level of design as part of the package. See page 72 for template site providers offering websites that can be set up today and trading tomorrow. Many e-commerce platform sites come with an in-built payment system. Here are the main ones.

PayPal

PayPal has more than 100 million active registered accounts and is available in 190 markets, meaning you can successfully trade in all these markets!

The company offers three main products: website payments standard, website payments pro and express checkout. To enable your customers to buy multiple items, use a free PayPal shopping cart. To put the 'Add to Cart' button on your website you simply copy and paste the HTML code from PayPal to the coding of your own site (bit.ly/blxrUn). Your customers then click the button to make a purchase. With PayPal, there are no set-up charges, monthly fees or cancellation charges, and fee levels vary depending on the volume of sales.

IN THE KIT

Pay just £1 per month for your website for the first three months – and no PayPal fees for the first 30 days – with EKM. Once the three months expire, you pay only £19.99 per month with no contract.

Google Checkout

Google Checkout (checkout.google.co.uk) is a global payment system. There are no set-up charges and fees depend on the volume of your sales. With monthly sales of less than £1,500, the fee is currently 3.4% plus 20p per transaction. This transaction fee decreases in line with sales volumes increasing.

Sage Pay

Sage Pay (www.sagepay.com) is a card payment service that allows you to accept payments by PayPal and major debit and credit cards. It is simple to manage and easy to integrate within your website. The fee is £20 per month for merchants processing up to 1,000 transactions per quarter and 10p per transaction for merchants processing more than 1,000 transactions per quarter, with a minimum charge of £20 per month. There are no set-up fees, no percentage fees and no annual charges.

Actinic (www.actinic.co.uk)	Actinic Express. £1 set-up fee and £15 per month thereafter for the bronze and basic package.	Company has been established in UK since 1996 and has built a solid reputation. Free 30-day trial on offer.
Big Cartel (www.bigcartel.com)	It's free to present five products, with monthly packages increasing to $29.99 per month for displaying up to 300 products.	With its strapline 'Bringing Art to the Cart', US-based Big Cartel has a focus on providing online stores for clothing designers, record labels, jewellers and crafters.
Create (www.create.net)	Packages start from £2.99 per month. 30-day free trial available.	Set up your site in minutes and benefit from email support plus online forums.
CubeCart (www.cubecart.com)	From free to £110, depending on the features required. Free 30-day trial on offer.	E-commerce shopping cart used by more than one million store owners – so they must be doing something right!
Moonfruit (www.moonfruit.com)	A basic site is free to build, moving up to £22.50 per month for premium options.	The company launched its most recent product Moonfruit Shopbuilder in October 2011, which automatically creates a store on Facebook and a mobile version of your site. The company has created 4.8 million sites.
MrSite (www.mrsite.com)	Three packages: £24.99 Beginner, £39.99 Standard, £99.99 Professional	You can buy the product in boxed or email format. Helpful tips on how to start via the site.
osCommerce (www.oscommerce.com)	Free	An open source solution with, to date, over 6,800 add-ons available for free to customise your store and increase sales.
SupaDupa (supadupa.me)	Price packages start free and then move through Plankton ($19 per month), Cod ($29 per month) and Caviar ($99 per month).	'Boutique e-commerce for creative minds' comes with the promise these sites will be easy to use and stylishly display your goods. You could spend a while on the main site browsing through what are beautiful looking boutiques.
Wix (www.wix.com)	A free build-your-site service with the ability to upgrade to premium plans that start at £10 per month.	Hundreds of designs to choose from and a drag and drop system to get you started.

MAKE YOUR WEBSITE LEGALLY COMPLIANT

These tips are offered by Joanna Tall, founder of
www.OfftoseemyLawyer.com

1. DISPLAY TERMS OF USE

"Think of your website like a board game you are about to play with your visitors. They arrive and are ready to play and you need to state the rules or else it will be chaos! So, for example, state what they can and cannot do – e.g. may they copy your materials? May they link to you? May they rely on the information you provide without double-checking with you or elsewhere? What liability are you prepared to accept? Provide a link to your terms of use, ideally on every page of your website or under a 'Legals' section.

2. DISPLAY YOUR PRIVACY POLICY

"Most websites collect personal data on their visitors either by getting them to register on the site or sign up for a newsletter. By law you must tell visitors what you will be doing with this data and the best way to do this is to set out the information in a privacy policy. Again, a link to it on every page is best. More complex rules apply if you plan to collect sensitive information or information from children, or want to pass the information to third parties; for this you should consult a lawyer. Additionally, you are likely to need to register as a data processor under the Data Protection Act. Simply go to **www.ico.gov.uk** for more information.

3. IF SELLING GOODS OR SERVICES ONLINE, DISPLAY YOUR TERMS OF SALE

"Just as with the board game example, you need rules for selling your goods or services. Most importantly, you need to get your visitors to acknowledge that they accept them. So ideally get them to tick a box stating that they accept them before they proceed to check out. You also need to draw their attention to their rights under the Distance Selling Regulations, e.g. cancellation rights amongst others.

4. PROTECT YOUR COPYRIGHT IN THE WEBSITE CONTENT

"Although you automatically own the copyright in the content that you create, best practice is to remind your visitors! Say, for example: "Copyright 2012 Lawyers R Great Ltd". And if your logo or name is trademarked, broadcast the fact! After all, you will have spent money in getting it that far and it will enhance your brand in the market.

5. STATE WHO YOU ARE!

"By law you need to state a full postal address and contact number and if you are a limited company, the company's registered address, number and country of registration. This also applies to your emails."

Distance Selling Regulations

One thing to bear in mind when selling goods or services to consumers via the internet, mail order or by phone, is compliance with the Consumer Protection (Distance Selling) Regulations 2000. The key features of the regulations are:

- You must offer consumers clear information including details of the goods or services offered, delivery arrangements and payment, the supplier's details and the consumer's cancellation rights before he or she buys (known as prior information). This information should be provided in writing.

- The consumer has a period of seven working days from delivery of the items to cancel their contract with you.

These regulations only apply when selling to consumers, as opposed to businesses. In the event of a contract being ceased, you have to refund money, including delivery charges, within 30 days of the date of cancellation.

- Distance Selling Regulations | **tinyurl.com/distancesellingregs**

3. A presence on other sites

Maybe you'd prefer to start raising your profile and making sales via other established platform sites, as opposed to your own. Whether selling homemade crafts or business concepts, there are a number of options.

The upside is that these sites attract customers on your behalf, and some of them attract customers from all over the world. Here are seven sales platforms that enable you to sell . . .

Alibaba

Having a presence on this site enables you to buy and sell with, and source supplies from, companies across the globe. The site has visitors from 240 countries and regions, with over 1 million registered users in the UK. Through the site you can locate suppliers or make sales of your finished product direct to customers. Alibaba is a champion of international trade; carrying out research on the topic, providing a platform for traders to interact, and promoting overseas sales as a form of business that is wholly viable, regardless of company size.

- www.alibaba.com | @AlibabaTalk_UK

The Forkan brothers turned to Alibaba when looking to source a supplier for their funky footwear brand . . .

CASE STUDY

NAME: **Rob and Paul Forkan** | BUSINESS: **Gandys**

Rob and Paul Forkan started their footwear company in 2011 using the brand name Gandys to sell stylish and fun flip-flops. Keeping it in the family, they brought in brother Matt to design the brand's logos, packaging and website. For these brothers in their early 20s, a key part of their business ethos is charitable action: they donate 10% of profits to an orphanage in Goa, India, with the long-term goal of building their own orphanage in the future. This vision is drawn from personal experience, having been orphaned themselves in the 2004 Boxing Day Tsunami.

With only the footwear idea and charitable vision in mind, the brothers set out to find the right manufacturer to help them build their ideal flip-flop. An online search led

Rob to Alibaba.com where he started building relationships with manufacturers.

"Starting out, we knew very little about how to source and manufacture our product. Thankfully, using Alibaba.com is as simple as using an online holiday-booking site. You enter your requirements and get a list of product manufacturers that suit your needs."

After working on prototypes with a few different suppliers, Gandys flip-flops were born. Six months later the brothers secured significant investment leading to the product being sold in 60 boutiques across Great Britain with plans to be in over 150 by summer 2013. Gandys are also in talks with a few major retailers.

To assist with expansion, Rob now uses Alibaba.com for more than sourcing the product:

"Most recently we sourced all of our point of sale for retailers on Alibaba.com. It's more competitive than purchasing within the UK. The site gives you the opportunity to shop around for the best prices; you can use it as a comparison tool. There is a wide variety of products and suppliers so you can find value and quality quickly."

Rob has visited China and India to meet suppliers but recommends others do as much as possible via Skype and email before investing in travel.

"You need to confirm everything with suppliers by sending diagrams and designs and repeating yourself a lot to make sure nothing is ever lost in translation. Even send examples and samples so you're sure of receiving the right end product. And I would say you only need to make sure the factory and everything is in line once you have orders."

Over the next 12 months the company is focused on developing relationships with major retailers in the UK, the US and Australia. The plan is to maintain a high profile (Gandys recently appeared in an Alibaba TV ad!) to try and fulfil the company's ambition of opening its first orphanage by 2014.

"What started out as a small project has now become something much more important. It has driven us to create a brand that is based on our beliefs and desire to do better in the world."

- www.gandysflipflops.com | @gandysflipflops

Amazon Marketplace

You may be used to buying from Amazon, but have you considered the site as a platform from which to sell? Have your products appear before millions of customers all around the world by signing up to Amazon Marketplace. It offers two sales options: a package for casual sellers who expect to sell less than 35 items a month (a fixed fee per sale plus a referral fee), and, for more seasoned sellers, there is the 'sell a lot' package, which has a monthly charge plus a referral fee for unlimited sales that do not have to be in the Amazon catalogue.

- www.amazon.co.uk/marketplace

eBay

In 2012 there were 190,000 registered businesses trading on eBay in the UK, generating billions of pounds-worth of sales. Having a store on eBay means you are opened up to an international audience and a lot of potential customers.

- www.eBay.co.uk

EBAY EXPERTISE

*Dan Wilson (**www.wilsondan.co.uk**) is an eBay author and co-editor of Tamebay, the highly popular eBay blog. Dan offers five tips on how to make the most of the mega marketplace:*

1. START SMALL

"Go slow until you've found your way. Start with a few, easy-to-post items and learn about eBay before boosting your range and prices. Don't stake too much on your first eBay bet.

2. SELL LIKE YOU MEAN IT

"The eBay marketplace is competitive and you'll lose out unless you have top-notch listings. Craft fabulous item titles, make impeccable pictures and write descriptions that tempt buyers. Be truthful and honest and look professional from the start.

3. BE QUICK OFF THE MARK

"Buyers have come to expect great service. Dispatch orders quickly — preferably within 24 hours of payment — and well packed, and make sure you reply to emails and other communications swiftly, too. The quality and speed of your replies and dispatches has an impact on customer feedback.

4. PUT A LID ON POSTAL COSTS

"Understand postage and packaging costs and make sure you factor it in to your costs where necessary.

5. LOYALTY MEANS PROFIT

"When you're building your eBay business, encouraging repeat buyers is important. Once a buyer trusts you as an online seller, they're likely to keep coming back. Offer discounts and incentives with every dispatch and cross-market complementary products."

Etsy

With its tag line 'Your place to buy and sell all things handmade' this is still the mother of all craft sites. Since the company launched in June 2005, more than 500,000 sellers from around the world have opened up Etsy shops and buyers of Etsy-listed products span more than 150 countries.

To start selling on Etsy you need to register for an account (this requires a credit card and valid email address for verification purposes) and then it costs 20 cents to list an item for four months. When your item sells, you pay a 3.5% transaction fee. For anyone who makes handmade items, the power of this global platform cannot be denied. Head a few pages on for a listing of handmade marketplaces you can try today.

- www.etsy.com | @etsy

Facebook

With more than 30 million users in the UK, a significant number of your present and potential customers spend time on Facebook every single day. If your business isn't there, it's missing out. Countless small business owners in the UK use Facebook to quickly and cost-effectively grow their company. The easiest way to start is through having an effective Facebook Page. Learn how to do this step by step in the free guide *Boost your Business with Facebook*, which also shows how to connect with new fans and make the most of Facebook ads.

- *Boost Your Business with Facebook* | www.enterprisenation.com/facebook-book-offer

iTunes

If you are a creator of audiobooks, a publisher of podcasts or developer of apps, then the iTunes platform is your route to market. For apps, Apple gives 70% of revenues to the seller. As of July 2011 over 15 billion apps had been downloaded from its App Store, making it the world's largest mobile application platform. Become a registered Apple developer for the iPhone (developer.apple.com/iphone) submit audio books to iTunes via Audible.com (www.audible.com) and create iBooks for the iPad through the iBookstore. Apple is opening up a world of opportunity for content creators and app developers.

- www.apple.com/itunes

Enterprise Nation Directory

Business support company Enterprise Nation has launched its own business directory to help its members promote their products and services. Premium members at Enterprise Nation get extra exposure in the directory, on the Enterprise Nation website, on Google, Twitter and Facebook. It's a great way to announce your start-up to a friendly business community – and connect with other small businesses too.

- www.enterprisenation.com/business-directory

IN THE KIT

Readers of *The StartUp Kit* can become premium members of Enterprise Nation for just £10 per year (half the normal price), and that includes one free business eBook per month and 25% off business events. Find out more at **www.enterprisenation.com/ premium** – and make sure you activate your kit to redeem your half-price offer.

HANDMADE marketplaces

A growing number of sites are dedicated to helping the young artisan and handmade business owner sell goods across the globe.

Etsy – www.etsy.com

"The world's handmade marketplace" (and a great place to start your selling).

How does it work?

1. You list the item on Etsy for a fee. It costs 20 cents (roughly 12p) to list an item for four months.

2. Shoppers then find your item, and purchase it from you directly, using your payment system which you have set up with Etsy. Etsy takes a 3.5% transaction fee from the total price of each sale.

3. You then ship the item directly to your customer.

Getting started

Setting up a shop on Etsy is easy and should only take a few minutes:
www.etsy.com/join

You will need to enter your Etsy username here, which will be displayed to customers looking at your products. Remember to think about your branding and how you want to present yourself to potential customers when entering these details.

Paying fees

All of your fees will be paid using the credit card you list when you register, or the PayPal account you link to your Etsy account. Etsy will calculate your fees on a monthly basis and email you with a list of payments that are due. You can also pay your bill manually through your account.

Community

Etsy has a thriving community where sellers, artists and creators all come together to share their work and ideas with one another. Etsy also run events such as Craft Nights, which could be a great way to meet other crafters and promote your products to a receptive audience.

The site has a blog which highlights new product launches and new initiatives, plus featured sellers and debates on various topics. Forums feature strongly on the site.

Not On The High Street –
www.notonthehighstreet.com

"One basket, hundreds of unique shops"

How does it work?

Not On The High Street offers you the chance to promote and sell your product under the umbrella of their brand and be supported by their in-house team. They look after all of the e-commerce, administration and marketing elements of selling through the site, so all you need to worry about are the products.

Not On The High Street differs from a number of other platform sites in that they are very selective about who sells with them and decline over 90% of applications. Membership packages vary but the basic package allows you to add 30 products to your own store, with your own logo, company name and URL.

Getting started

If you're interested in getting set up with NOTHS, you will need to take some photographs of your products and submit these using the online application form.

Applications can take up to seven working days to be processed. After that time you will be contacted by a member of the team.

Folksy – www.folksy.com

"Folksy is a place to buy handmade things, and for makers to sell their work and find supplies. Based in the UK, Folksy aims to reclaim craft and showcase talented makers and their work."

You can sell craft supplies on Folksy as well as handmade goods, so long as they are listed as 'supplies' and not in the 'handmade' category.

How does it work?

1. It costs 20p to list an item for 180 days or until the item is sold.

2. Shoppers purchase from you directly, using your payment system which you have set up with Folksy, for example PayPal, or you can accept other payments, such as cash or cheques at your own discretion. Folksy takes a 5% commission fee from the total value of each sale.

3. You then ship the item directly to your customer.

Getting started

The first thing you need to do is decide on the username for your shop. This can't be changed so think carefully about your branding and how you want to appear to prospective customers.

Once your item is listed, customers can start viewing and purchasing. When an order is received you will get an order from Folksy with all the buyer's details and the information about the product ordered. You will also receive notification to say payment has been completed. You then ship the product directly to the customer.

Paying fees

You settle fees through the Your Account section of the website. The total shown will be made up of billed and unbilled fees as well as the 5% commission on sales.

Community

Folksy features a blog which gives updates on important news and events. The site also has a forum where members can discuss craft tips, as well as events, ideas for your shopfront and anything else that takes your fancy!

DaWanda – en.dawanda.com

"DaWanda is the place for unique and individual products and people. Buy handmade and hard to find goods, share your discoveries with your friends and create your own collections."

How does it work?

List your items on the site and set up your own shop which gives you the option of a direct URL – nice and easy to promote to your customers!

People will browse your listings and when someone orders a product you receive an email. You check the details of the order, making a note of any special requests from the buyer, and once happy to go ahead you click to confirm the order, so the buyer can see the final price and pay you. You then ship the item directly to the customer using the method you have specified in the listing.

Getting started

With DaWanda you can set up your own shop for free – all you need to do is provide a name and set up shop categories. You can create your own shop window at this stage to show off the key items in your shop. As soon as this has been established, you can start listing your items and selling to customers!

DaWanda also features something called the DaWanda widget, a tool for displaying your shop on your own website or blog.

Paying fees

DaWanda charges a 5% commission on all sales but does not charge for listing products. Once your fees reach €5, DaWanda will email you an invoice with instructions on how to pay.

Community

The website features the News Bulletin Board as well as a blog, ideal for getting all the latest information on what DaWanda offers and what's popular on the site. The forums are a great place to chat with other crafters and there are also video, social media and Gift Detective areas.

ArtFire –
www.artfire.com

"The Premier handmade marketplace to buy and sell handmade crafts, supplies, vintage and art"

How does it work?

Set up your shop and list as many items as you want, with up to 10 photographs per item.

The customer will browse your shop and place an order. You receive the customer's payment and also their delivery details in order to ship the product.

Getting started

You can set up your shop for free at – **www.artfire.com/ext/register/account**.

You then pay nothing for 30 days, and after that the rate is a £7.56 a month for unlimited listings. ArtFire do not take a commission on sales.

Paying fees

Fees will be taken from your nominated payment card on the same day each month (the one on which you originally signed up). For example, if you joined on the 5th December, you would be charged your monthly fee on the 5th of every month.

Community

ArtFire has a range of different community options for you to get involved in and interact with other members. There are forums where you can communicate and share ideas with other crafters, as well as ArtDaily, which is an opportunity to learn new crafts and get sound business advice, plus there's the chance to join a guild and earn a guild badge, as well as listen to the weekly podcast from John Jacobs and Tony Ford, giving tips on how to promote your business and use ArtFire to its full potential.

MISI (Make It, Sell It) – www.misi.co.uk

"The home of buying and selling handmade in the UK"

How does it work?

Create a shop with MISI and list your items for free. When you sell a product you will receive an email notification from MISI which will prompt you to log in to see the full details of the sale. Payment can either be by cheque or PayPal, and once payment is received, you ship the product direct to the customer.

Paying fees

MISI charges 20p per listing, which will be added to your account as soon as you start listing items. MISI also take a 3% commission fee on every sale and this is also added to your account. Fees are then payable on a monthly basis.

Community

The MISI community section is broken down into several areas including: a blog where crafters write about their latest ideas, materials and events; a forum for sharing tips and ideas; and a Meet the Maker section where shop-owners and crafters are encouraged to share their experiences with the community.

ShopHandmade – www.shophandmade.com

"Rewarding Creativity"

How does it work?

You can sell your items in five easy steps! Once you have listed your products, customers can browse them and begin buying right away. When an item sells, you're notified by email, and payment is made to your registered PayPal account. You then ship the item using easy-to-print labels from PayPal.

Getting started

List your item for a small fee of 25 cents, and then upload up to five photos per item. Then you need to decide if you are participating in Sales and Galleries and activate your listing.

When you are listing items, there is also the opportunity to get the listing sponsored, which means a third-party sponsor will pay for listing your item, costing you nothing. There are several sponsors to choose from and their sponsorship simply means that a non-intrusive advertisement will appear on your product page.

Paying fees

ShopHandmade only charge a percentage of an item's final selling price. The payment is taken when an item actually sells.

Community

ShopHandmade features blogs from various sellers so that you can see what other crafters are up to and keep track of developments and new ideas in the crafting world.

A TOP QUALITY IMAGE: Whether you decide to start online with a blog or a full e-commerce site, place high quality images on your site and printed materials so that on first click or at first glance, a customer is inclined to buy. Take professional images yourself or consider subscribing to a stock image library such as www.istockphoto.com. Other image libraries include: www.imagesource.com, www.photos.com and www.gettyimages.com. Search for Creative Commons licensed images you can use commercially from Flickr at www.compfight.com.

CASE STUDY

NAME: **Alyssa Williamson** | **BUSINESS:** **Peach Blossom**

After leaving university, Alyssa Williamson had trouble finding the type of job she wanted to do long-term – so she decided to create her own dream job by starting her own business: Peach Blossom, a party accessories supplier.

Whilst working as a receptionist, Alyssa would dedicate time at nights and weekends to preparing a business plan, setting up a website, and researching the products she was going to sell.

"I've always been interested in event and party planning. When I planned my own events I couldn't find the kind of products I wanted, so I knew there was a gap for something new and exciting."

Early on, Alyssa decided to join online marketplace notonthehighstreet.com, which provided a great boost to the business.

"Via my own site and through Notonthehighstreet (NOTHS) I've had orders all across the UK and internationally. NOTHS has been a great way of increasing sales as it broadens my online presence. Although I am responsible for all the orders I get through the site and for communicating with customers, NOTHS has been great in offering advice in improving sales."

Peach Blossom has gone on to be featured in magazines, newspapers and blogs, bringing national exposure and sales.

"Twitter and Facebook have played a big part, too, as they're a great way of connecting with customers, journalists and other businesses."

To keep the product line fresh, Alyssa attends trade shows and does a lot of online research. With a good knowledge of the party industry Alyssa knows where to look for new products but also feels it's important to keep an eye on trends to anticipate the products that will keep customers interested.

The business is growing and Alyssa is grateful for strong support from her family who get involved when it comes to setting up at events and processing orders, or simply offering advice.

"I'm also really lucky that my mum has a background in finance so she does the accounts for the business."

With promotion, support and sales underway, Alyssa is confident about the future and looking to expand in both retail and wholesale sectors.

"I also have lots of ideas for products I would like to create, so a new collection of Peach Blossom products is in the works. Watch this space!"

● **www.peachblossom.co.uk** | @peachblossomuk

Rise up the search engine ranks

Promote your business and website through search engine optimisation. Commonly referred to as SEO, this is the process by which you can improve rankings for your website in the top search engines such as Google, so that your site appears on the first few pages of results rather than on page 75.

Google is a search engine that uses software known as 'spiders' to crawl the web on a regular basis and find sites to add to their index. There are steps you can take to make it easier for the spiders to find and add your site.

THINK LIKE A BUYER: When thinking of the keywords to use in PPC (pay per click) ad campaigns (and in search engine optimisation) think of the words your buyers will be using when searching for your product or service. Use the Google AdWords Keyword Tool to find out the most popular search terms. Apply these words in the campaign and include them in the text on your site.

Start with the homepage

Provide high-quality, text-based content on your pages – especially your homepage. If your homepage has useful information and good quality, relevant text, it's more likely to be picked up by the spiders. Beyond the homepage, write pages that clearly describe your topic/service/product. Think about the words users would type to find your pages and include them on the site.

Make contributions

Identify influential bloggers and sites in your trade/industry, contact them and offer to write posts. You can also improve your visibility by writing helpful comments in forums and on other people's posts.

Be well connected

Improve the rank of your site by increasing the number of other high-quality sites that link to your pages; these are referred to as inbound links. For example, if you're running a competition, go to sites that promote competitions and add yours.

Register your site with the major search engines.

- Google | www.google.co.uk/addurl
- Yahoo! | search.yahoo.com/info/submit
- Bing | www.bing.com/webmaster/submitsitepage.aspx

SEARCH ENGINES LOVE LINKS: Another way to increase your ranking in the search results is to link to other sites and vice versa, but think quality here as opposed to quantity. Sites offering the best 'link juice' are trusted domains, such as news sites, and very popular sites. You could post comments on such sites and blogs and include a link back to your site. Try these handy hints: approach sites complementary to your own and suggest reciprocal links; ensure that your website link is included in all your social media profiles; register with the major search engines (see above); add your domain to local search services such as Google Maps, Qype, Yahoo! Local and BView.

- www.google.co.uk/maps
- www.qype.co.uk
- www.uk.local.yahoo.com

Tagging

A webpage's title, referred to as a 'title tag', is part of the SEO mix and can make a difference to your search rankings. It is also the text that appears in the top of the browser window. Include in your title tag the main key phrase you'd like the search engines to associate with your webpage and keep it to 60-90 characters in length. Duncan Green of Moo Marketing is an SEO expert and explains: "the title tag on the homepage for Moo Marketing reads: 'Moo Marketing – Search Engine Marketing – PPC Management – Search Engine Optimisation'. As you can see the title element is 85 characters long, contains three key phrases and identifies the subject of the webpage."

Pay per click advertising

The results from your efforts in SEO will appear on the main engines as a natural or 'organic' search result. But have you spotted results on the right of the page when searching for items yourself? These are paid-for results and referred to as pay per click or PPC advertising. PPC is where you pay to have ads displayed when people type in certain words, in the hope it will attract more visitors to your site.

Google AdWords is a form of PPC advertising. Think of the key words or phrases you reckon your customers will be searching for and apply them in your Google campaign. Link to your home page or other pages on the site where you're running a promotion and make the most of geotargeting, which lets you target your ads to specific territories and languages. You are in full control of the budget and campaign duration.

- adwords.google.co.uk

Spread the word

Make it easy for visitors to spread word of your site through social sharing. Have your site Stumbled, Dugg and Tweeted and make the most of this viral effect. You can add these social bookmarking tools by visiting AddThis (**www.addthis.com**) and choosing the icons you'd like to have displayed on your site.

The most popular are:

- Delicious | **www.delicious.com**
- Digg | **www.digg.com**
- StumbleUpon | **www.stumbleupon.com**

Your business in print

Print is far from dead, so get yourself some business cards, postcards and promotion flyers to hand out at business events, social occasions, and to just about anyone you meet! Have fun with designing your cards at www.moo.com and get a range of designs printed in each batch. Sell vintage fashion? Upload pictures of your products to the reverse of each card. Offer web design services? Have a portfolio of sites you've designed there.

IN THE KIT

Get 50 Classic or Green Business cards from **moo.com** for free.

Look at my logo!

When you contact potential customers you'll want them to read about you and get a sense of your style. You can do this very effectively with a nice-looking logo or company design that's repeated across all your promotion materials, from business cards to brochures.

Think about what you'd like as your company font, colours and layout. Have a go at designing this yourself or hire the services of a designer/neighbour/friend. Good presentation can make a world of difference. This may just be the difference you need to clinch a contract.

Find a professional to design your logo via these sites:

- Enterprise Nation Directory | www.enterprisenation.com/business-directory
- CrowdSPRING | www.crowdspring.com
- 99designs | www.99designs.com
- BuildaBrand | www.buildabrand.com
- Concept Cupboard | www.conceptcupboard.com
- oDesk | www.odesk.com

Office address

If you are running the business from home there are a couple of reasons why you might not want to put the home address on your business card: it might sound too domestic, and you might not want people turning up on your doorstep!

You can solve this with a P.O. Box number, which starts at £185 per year and is easily set up with Royal Mail (www.royalmail.com/pobox). Alternatively, you could invest in a virtual office, which gives you a more tailored and personal service than a P.O. Box – plus you get a nice-sounding address and a place to use for meetings. Having a virtual office enables you to choose the address that suits you best, have post delivered to that location, and then forwarded on to you. Companies providing this service include:

- Regus | www.regus.co.uk
- Bizspace | www.bizspace.co.uk

When holding meetings, consider hiring professional meeting space. Many offer serviced addresses and secretarial services too, so there could be great continuity for your clients if they only have to remember one address.

IN THE KIT

Get one month's free virtual office or one month free in any Bizspace unit.

Get a value business start-up package from Regus, including impressive business address, call answering, mail-handling, business mentoring, drop-in business lounges and more.

Get 'Three Days, One Club' Membership at Kennington Park, Enterprise House or Barley Mow reduced to £150+VAT pcm for the first three months from Club Workspace.

On the phone

When running the business from home, consider who will be picking up the phone! It's cheap and sometimes free to get an 0845 local rate number or an 0870 national rate number for your business. This will hide where you're based and divert your calls to wherever you specify. But beware: sometimes having such a number – especially with national rates – might put customers off ringing you.

If you use a landline number it's best to have a separate line for your home and your business. These days you don't need to invest in an actual second line. You can use a VoIP (voice over internet protocol) phone, which uses a broadband internet connection to make and receive calls, something we looked at earlier.

- Skype | www.skype.com

Another idea is to get some help from a call-handling service. They will answer your calls with your company name, text urgent messages to you and email the others, giving you a big business feel for about £50 per month. Services on offer include:

- Moneypenny | www.moneypenny.co.uk
- Regus | www.regus.co.uk
- MyRuby | www.myruby.co.uk
- Answer | www.answer.co.uk

You might consider a 'follow-me number' to ensure you're available when you need to be and able to deliver the right impression to clients. A follow-me number involves choosing a number and directing calls from it to your landline or mobile. The beauty of choosing a number is that you have the option to select either a freephone or a geographical number so, say you'd like to have a Manchester area code, simply buy a number starting with 0161. The same goes for hundreds of other locations.

Offer virtual phone numbers where the caller pays a local rate, regardless of where you are, through Vonage (www.vonage.co.uk) or direct calls to you from a chosen number using internet technology and a virtual receptionist at eReceptionist (www.ereceptionist.co.uk).

In person

You are about to attend your first networking event or trade show and want to create a good first impression. With an attractive business card in hand, directing prospective customers to a good-looking online presence, all you have to do is follow the rules of effective networking!

The art of networking

- Wear your name tag (if you have one) on your right side. It's easy to catch sight of when you are shaking hands.

- Deliver a nice firm handshake and make eye contact.

- Say your name clearly and, in under ten seconds, tell the other person who you are and what you do.

- Listen carefully. Ask the other person plenty of questions about their line of business, their hobbies, etc.

- Be positive and energetic.

- Swap business cards.

- Send a thank-you email after the event, confirming any actions you and they have promised.

- Keep in regular and meaningful contact.

See Chapter 12 for details of networking groups to join and for information on how to host your own event or attend a trade show to promote your business.

A MEMORABLE EXCHANGE: Richard Moross, founder of moo.com, says: "The point of having a business card is to make a connection, create a relationship and leave something with the recipient that reminds them of you. Have cards that tell a story. Use that card as a sales tool, for sure, but also show appreciation by having cards relating to your customer." Richard achieves this by having images on his cards showing places he's visited and meals he's eaten. With 70% of moo.com's business being outside the UK, Richard travels a lot and the cards act as the ice-breaker in meetings as he tells the story behind the pictures.

11. MAKE SALES

With a professional image established, you are ready to start making sales. This chapter will help you achieve that first sale, plus provide tips on how to make money from your website or blog.

1. Make a list (check it twice)

Draw on your existing resources, grab your address book and select the friends, family, colleagues and acquaintances you think might be interested in your product or service. Add to the list with details of local people and businesses, too.

2. Pitch up

Contact the people on your list and announce your new business venture. Consider this an opportunity to make your pitch, but don't be too pushy. Remember to address each recipient personally. No one likes a group email!

3. Follow up

Follow up in a few days time, either with another email or, better still, a phone call. Take some soundings as to the success of your pitch and react accordingly. If the potential customer or client sounds keen, go for it! Arrange to meet him or her to show your product or explain more about your service.

4. Meet up

Arrange a time and place to meet that's convenient for your potential customer or client. Be professional, but also likeable. These are equally important characteristics when making a sale.

If the customer agrees the deal, bring the meeting to a fairly speedy end. Your job is done – for now. It's time to head home and deliver on the promise you made with your first customer.

5. Make some noise

Once you've made your first sale – shout about it! If your new customer or client agrees, include them in a press release or write about them on your website or blog, so other potential customers or clients can see that you're well and truly in business!

SALES ARE FLYING HIGH: Have promotional flyers made to take to events or deliver through doors. Increase chances of turning flyers into firm sales by:

- having a design that is memorable, possibly quirky and, ideally, that your potential customers will want to keep on their desk/in their bag/atop the kitchen shelf

- making the offer clear and confirming the benefits of buying

- including a call to action, i.e. a way in which the interested customer can contact you.

Warm up for a cold call

*Sales and marketing pro Jackie Wade (**www.winningsales.co.uk**) offers tips on how to make winning calls to customers . . .*

"**Ready:** Preparation and focus is key. Start with a call list and clear objectives; which business or household and who specifically are you calling (decision maker)? Are you clear on your message? What benefits do you offer?

"**Steady:** Feel confident, think positive. What's the worst thing that can happen? They may say no... so what! Not everyone out there will want you, but someone will! Tone is more important than words so feel and sound confident and positive.

"**Go:** Be natural, be you. Have a good opening 'hook' to grab attention – something interesting, new or different and make it relevant to the person you're calling. Avoid rambling – focus on a two-way conversation, not a fixed script. Develop a list of open questions which will allow you to engage with the person at the other end of the line, e.g. what do you currently do, how does it work, what might you like to improve? Listen for opportunities. Engage!

"**Grow:** Agree action and follow up promptly or agree a call back, if no interest for now. A NO today may be a YES tomorrow; tenacity counts. Things change.

"Remember, smile and then dial. Your aim is to spread the word about you and your business."

WHEN MAKING A SALES CALL, do so standing up and smiling. To the person on the other end, you will come across as positive and confident.

Selling into physical stores

Maybe you've started by selling products direct to customers at shows and fairs, but what about making sales via local shops?

Before you approach any shops, make a list of appropriate places where you think your product could work well. For example, does your town have gift shops or an art gallery, are there lots of boutiques that stock a range of different items? Think outside the box. Could your local coffee shop stock some of your items?

Five top tips for market placement

Laura Rigney, founder of Pitcher House, is author of *Pitching Products for Small Business* and offers five top tips for pitching your product effectively:

1. Be confident with pricing

"Selling in wholesale is a whole new ballpark as far as pricing is concerned. Make your product attractive to buyers with your pricing. A great way to show you're trying to help retailers is to setup a structured pricing system, i.e. 100 units or less £xx per unit, 101-500 units £xx per unit and 501 units or more £xx per unit. This system could also encourage shops and buyers to place larger orders.

2. Understand your product inside out

"This means technical data as well as knowing why someone would buy it. When you get a meeting with a buyer or approach a shop owner, talk with confidence about where the product is made, by who, and using what kind of materials. Remember there is pressure on large retailers to "go green", so the more you can offer that as a potential supplier the more attractive you will be.

3. Be prepared

"If a buyer places an order, how quickly will you have manufacturing, distribution and storage in place? Buyers won't expect a new small business to have a giant factory sitting waiting for someone to press the 'go' button but they will want a realistic estimate of how long it will be until your product is in their warehouses/on the shop shelf. Once you have given your timings, stick to them. Even if this means exaggerating the time it will take for them to be delivered. Better to be early rather than late!

4. Pitch perfect

"If you're pitching in person, make it informative, exciting and interesting and where possible have evidence of past sales and customer satisfaction. You need to know your figures without having to look through paperwork and be prepared to haggle a little on prices. If someone likes your product enough and you have sold it well enough they will buy it, even if it's a few pennies more than they would like to pay. In the other direction, sometimes it may be worth offering a larger than normal discount as a trial for a first order.

5. Stay listed

"When a company takes on your product it's called being listed. Once you are listed the work is just beginning! It is now time to stay listed for as long as possible and the way to do this is through marketing and PR. The more you promote your product and the shops/galleries/boutiques that are selling them, the more they will be bought by consumers thus encouraging buyers to place more orders with you!"

PITCHUP! Apply to StartUp Britain's PitchUp project to have your products placed in front of national buyers. Shortlisted contenders get the opportunity to meet with retailers such as John Lewis and be in with a chance of securing a contract. www.startupbritain.co/highstreet

Donnie Maclean has applied his entrepreneurial skills – with help from friends – to get his products stocked in Asda and Sainsbury's. He's the man who's re-inventing the pizza and attracting attention from across the globe . . .

CASE STUDY

NAME: **Donnie Maclean** | BUSINESS: **Eat Balanced**

Eat Balanced is a business that is re-inventing the pizza. The idea came from what Donnie Maclean describes as an evolutionary process, rather than a light bulb moment.

"I had been trying to ensure I was getting a properly balanced diet to improve my performance in triathlons. This led me to identify a few opportunities for a business. I tapped into several experts in the space (professors and doctors of nutrition) and got on well with one of the professors and we threw a few ideas around. I suggested trying to make a pizza a complete balanced meal, and he liked it, so we investigated it further and struck it lucky!"

Donnie has been helped along the way by being part of Entrepreneurial Spark (**www.entrepreneurial-spark.com**), a business accelerator in Glasgow.

"Being a part of Entrepreneurial Spark has been instrumental to our success because it has pushed me up a gear or two. Their main motto is *go do* – essentially, don't just think about something, take action! There is such a positive energy here in 'The Hatchery' and the founder, Jim Duffy, along with the full Entrepreneurial Spark team have been supportive of our business from the start."

Donnie has even sealed a deal to have his product on the shelves (well, in the freezers) of Sainsbury's and Asda.

"When we attended the Scotland Food & Drink Awards, I chatted to the host for the evening and had a laugh with him. I told him about my business. He loved the idea so much that he gave me two mentions in his opening speech. This caught the attention of the supermarket buyers who were all keen to speak with me at the end of the night. Tactical networking! We didn't even win an award, but everyone was talking about us."

This led to meetings for Donnie and his sales director with the frozen buyer for both Sainsbury's and Asda who immediately took to the concept, packaging and product taste.

"With any new food product, the chances of success in the supermarkets are slim. I've been able to consolidate the initial interest by bringing in a top-class sales director, who has excellent experience with the supermarkets, and has defended our position once we were in there. This experience and credibility is invaluable, and significantly strengthens the potential for this new business."

Not resting on his laurels with contracts under his belt, Donnie and the Eat Balanced team are hard at work promoting the business.

"We focus on marketing activities in a number of areas to reach our target audience, whilst trying to keep costs down by being as savvy as possible."

Marketing has taken place through entering and winning awards, leading to national press and profile. The company has also embraced social media, interacting with followers on Twitter and hosting competitions on Facebook. A forthcoming video is planned for the site as well as work on product endorsements and sponsorships, sending product samples to journalists, creating eye-catching designs that differentiate the Eat Balanced packaging on the shelves, and in-store sampling and exhibitions.

This activity was given a boost in July 2012 when the company was featured on the BBC.

"It was the second most shared article on the BBC news website and from this the story was covered worldwide. It was brilliant!"

Donnie has travelled a long way without raising any external funds or investment. Watch this space for developments in that area, as well as the launch of new product ranges, international expansion and more sales in stores.

The only complaint this business owner has about work and life right now?

"Lots of ideas, too little time!"

- www.eatbalanced.com | @eatbalanced

PopUps

Want to hone retail skills, meet customers face to face and make sales? Why not try a high street PopUp and test new markets in the flesh?

PopUp Britain (www.popupbritain.co.uk) was created to give new British brands an opportunity to get onto the high street and fill empty shops with small business activity. The flagship PopUp store in Richmond opened in July 2012 and has since welcomed start-ups and small businesses who trade in the shop for a fortnight before moving on to allow new businesses to move in.

The PopUp tenants are all online businesses that don't normally have the budget to take on a shop single-handedly and full time. PopUp Britain brings tenants together to share the cost and workload. Following success in Richmond, the scheme is expanding across the UK.

The project has delivered a national 'PopUp Lease' (thanks to Nick Darby at SNR Denton) which makes contractual arrangements with landlords a whole lot simpler. And with support from Minister for Housing and High Streets, Mark Prisk, a PopUp should be coming to a town near you soon.

Edoardo Cannarsa tells how he benefited from a PopUp experience and on page 162 you can read a profile of the We Are Pop Up team (www.wearepopup.com) who are building a platform to match willing landlords and interested tenants.

The art of the pop

Here's how to ensure your PopUp experience is a profitable one.

- Place – choose a shop in a location that suits your products and is populated with people who represent your target market.

- Offer – ahead of moving into the shop, prepare sufficient stock at a price that's right for the particular area. Present the produce in a way that will attract customers' attention. Consider your own presentation and body language when approaching and dealing with customers.

- Promote – now you're in the shop, tell people you're there! Promote your presence to existing customers through social media. To attract new trade, consider partnerships with neighbouring retailers, flyers in the train station, releases to the local press and PopUp parties, lock-ins, cook-offs and fashion shows, to deliver a retail experience that customers will never forget!

Get the POP right and you'll see sales and profile on the UP!

CASE STUDY

NAME: **Edoardo Cannarsa** | BUSINESS: **MyEdo**

Have you ever met a man who made his first online sale without having told anyone the site existed? Well, in this profile you will – his name is Edoardo Cannarsa, founder of luxury fashion company MyEdo.

"I started trading in October 2011 under the brand name of MyEdo as a blazer jacket specialist, offering classic Italian wear for the modern man and woman. My first online client came one day after the site went live, and was from South Africa – with no SEO, PR or promotion of any kind! I thought I had hit the jackpot but later discovered the buyer was someone who had heard about the site via referral from a friend on Facebook. This customer loved the designs, wasn't able to purchase such garments in his own country, and spent over £500 on the first order. That was the start of MyEdo!"

Before starting the business Edoardo had worked for an IT reseller in a sales and account management role. But fashion was his passion, and with a mother based in Italy who had a background in the trade, Edoardo was drawn into the business.

"My mother is an influential part of the business as she lives in Italy from where I source my collection. She helps with buying and meets the brands. She calls straightaway if she spots any new designs that will suit my customers. Thanks to Skype she can show me the products so I don't need to buy lots of plane tickets to Italy!"

Edoardo was keen to showcase styles and designs to customers in person but not being able to afford space on the high street, he partnered with clubs and bars and hosted events in offices which resulted in a few sales.

Edoardo then applied to be a tenant in the PopUp Britain shop in Richmond during a themed fortnight for luxury fashion brands.

"The PopUp experience was a game-changer. We made a fantastic amount of sales, more than I had expected. I had been so heavily fixated on marketing, SEO and driving traffic to the website that I had overlooked the potential of showing my products on the high street. It changed the way I play the game. I see the PopUp route as an extra string to my bow, something I can't ignore – and something I have to keep doing in the future."

Bitten by the PopUp bug, this stylish business owner is now planning more London PopUps. And if these are successful, the plan is to expand to Manchester, Liverpool and Birmingham.

Maybe you'll see Edoardo appearing in a town near you soon!

- **www.myedo.co.uk** | @MyEdoCoUk

Going global

Of the 18 businesses profiled in this kit, 70% are trading overseas; making sales via the platform sites or selling directly into new markets through local contacts and/or assistance from UK Trade & Investment.

To discover more about the specifics of international trade and how to go global in five basic steps, download a free eBook (tinyurl.com/goglobalguide) which offers all you need to know on topics from customs documentation to website translation and perfecting the art of cultural etiquette.

- *Go Global* eBook | **tinyurl.com/goglobalguide**
- Go Global on Enterprise Nation | **tinyurl.com/goglobalEN**
- DHL blog | **www.dhlguide.co.uk/blog**
- UK Trade & Investment | **www.ukti.gov.uk**
- Alibaba | **www.alibaba.com**

In her first year of trading Sally Guyer sold more of her product overseas than in the UK. And promotion was all through social media . . .

CASE STUDY

NAME: **Sally Guyer** | BUSINESS: **Cambridge Raincoat Company**

Sally Guyer has a part-time job teaching English to international students. The rest of the time she runs her business, Cambridge Raincoat Company, designing and selling coats.

The initial idea was a stylish solution for cyclists – beautifully designed fashion items that would be breathable, wind-proof, washable, water resistant and durable. But Sally saw items from both her men and women's range become all-year-round fashionable pieces.

"Being made in Britain is still synonymous with quality and being classy. My first sale was to the USA, thanks to the reach of the internet. In the first year of trading I sold more overseas than I did in the UK. The coats weigh less than a kilo and I post them myself. Promotion has largely been through Twitter and Facebook. I also won £15,000-worth of local advertising in January 2012 which has helped a lot with local promotion, as you can imagine!"

Sally plans to continue with the international push and has been approached by potential agents in Germany and China who only deal with British-made goods. Her ultimate ambition is to have the business turning over sufficient income so that she can give up the part-time job and focus full time on what is already a global business!

● www.cambridgeraincoats.co.uk | @cantala59

Make money from your website

As traffic to your blog increases, so does your chance of generating income. Make a profit from your posts with this top-ten list of options.

1. Display advertising

Offer advertising on your site. The more niche your audience, the more likely you are to attract advertisers.

The information you'll need to provide includes:

- number of unique visitors
- number of impressions
- average duration of visit
- visitor demographics.

Write a basic rate card (see a few pages' time), add it to your site and send it to corporate marketing departments and media-buying agencies.

2. Google AdSense

This tool from Google does the work for you by placing relevant ads on your site and earning you money when people click on them. You can customise the appearance of the ads so they sit well with the style of your site.

- www.google.co.uk/adsense

3. Text Link Ads

These ads offer direct click-throughs from text on your site. You submit your site to Text Link Ads and then upload the ad code provided. It's your choice whether you approve or deny the supplied ads. Once that's done, you start making money as visitors click on the ads. Try this and Skimlinks, which converts words on your site to affiliate links so that you earn from those, too.

- www.text-link-ads.com
- www.skimlinks.com

4. Sponsored conversations

Get paid for posts (and now tweets) with services like IZEA that match bloggers with advertisers. Some doubt the ethical stance of paying a blogger to write something about a product but there's no doubt that it's a money maker.

- www.izea.com

5. Affiliate schemes

Sign up to affiliate schemes like the Amazon Associates Programme, where you can earn up to 10% in referrals by advertising Amazon products. The programme works by driving traffic to Amazon.co.uk through specially formatted links. You earn referral fees on sales generated through those links. Monthly cheques are sent to you from Amazon and it's easy and free to join.

- affiliate-program.amazon.co.uk

6. Sponsored features

This could include a host of options. Approach advertisers with suggestions of a sponsored eBook, e-news, podcast, webchat, poll or survey. These applications can be added to your site at a low cost yet generate good revenue.

For:

- eBook creation, try www.blurb.com
- a survey or poll feature, try www.surveymonkey.com
- email marketing, try www.mailchimp.com

7. Expert help

Offer your expertise and charge people to log on and watch or listen. This could be made available through Teleclasses where you invite customers and contacts onto a call where you offer your expertise on a one-to-many basis. Or deliver a presentation to potentially thousands of paying customers via www.gotowebinar.co.uk.

8. Deals with suppliers

Do deals with suppliers. Hosting a travel blog? Agree a percentage each time a booking is made via your site. Hosting a wedding blog? Create a directory of wedding suppliers such as venues, photographers, dressmakers and caterers with an enhanced listing for those who pay.

9. Turn a blog into a book

Follow the lead of Alex Johnson who turned his Shedworking blog (www.shedworking.co.uk) into a book – and then a second book – which are now selling across the UK and overseas, acting as an effective marketing tool for the site!

10. Please donate

If you'd rather just ask for a small donation from your visitors, this is possible too via a donate feature from PayPal. Add a PayPal donate button to your site: bit.ly/ikf832

* * *

Maybe you've decided to start selling products through your site. But if you only carry content, you'll need to add an e-commerce feature to make sales.

JUST-IN-TIME PAYMENT: Add a PayPal payment button to your site and you'll be able to accept payment from all major credit and debit cards, as well as bank accounts around the world. You can set it up in less than 15 minutes.

Add an e-commerce plug-in

Want to open your site up to sales? Do so by plugging in an e-commerce tool such as:

- WordPress e-Commerce shopping cart – "suitable for selling your products, services, or fees online": bit.ly/fEgQHo

- PayPal Shortcodes – insert PayPal buttons in your posts or pages using a Shortcode: bit.ly/KGNE5f

- View a complete list of WordPress e-commerce plugins: bit.ly/eTEkwZ

Add a shopping cart to your site

Make it easy for your visitors to click and buy. Check out these shopping cart providers:

- GroovyCart | www.groovycart.co.uk

- RomanCart | www.romancart.com

- CubeCart | www.cubecart.com

- Zen Cart | www.zen-cart.com

- ekmPowershop | www.ekmpowershop.com

- osCommerce | www.oscommerce.com

- Frooition | www.frooition.com [shopping cart and full website]

Research the product that suits you best, taking into account hosting provision, back-end admin, and built-in search engine optimisation. For more information on e-commerce, view the video series '10 steps to e-commerce success' produced by Enterprise Nation in association with PayPal: www.enterprisenation.com/e-commerce-videos

SHOW ME YOUR RATES! The purpose of a media rate card is to show potential advertisers what your site can deliver to them in terms of traffic and sales. To do this, include some key points:

- **A brief description of the site:** What it does and for whom.

- **Visitor demographics:** Do you have data on the age of your visitors, their home region, gender, etc? If so, include it, as it helps build a picture of your audience.

- **Site traffic:** What are your unique visitor numbers and length of time spent on the site? Make a note if the figures are increasing.

- **Costings:** Do you have a cost-per-click (CPC) or cost-per-impression (CPM) rate? If so, include it here, along with the price of other sponsorship options. Offer a menu but leave some flexibility, with 'costed on a project basis' for sponsor features that would benefit from a more tailored proposal.

- **Screen shots:** Showing how and where adverts or sponsored features appear on the site.

- **Media activity:** Note where you've recently been covered in the media, online and off, so that potential sponsors can see how and where you're promoting the site.

- **Testimonials:** Positive comments from existing sponsors gives you credibility and gives confidence to the next potential sponsor.

- **Team details:** Who are the faces behind the site and what are their credentials? In other words, your background career and activities, etc.

Round this off with your contact details so that interested potential sponsors can get in touch and place an order!

12. MAKE SOME NOISE!

Sales are coming in, customers are happy and you want to tell the world about you and your new business. Profile brings new customers and new sales. Get yourself known in the press and online by making friends with the media, hosting events, entering awards and embracing social media.

Here's what to do.

Plot the script

Imagine yourself as the star of your own Hollywood movie. Are you an action hero, battling against the odds (think James Dyson) or a brand leading lady (think Nigella Lawson)? Plot the action and write the script. It will help you define your message to the media.

Find the right contacts

Research the journalists you think are interested in your field. Note their email addresses from the bottom of their articles, follow them on Twitter, get to know them and send them exclusive stories about you and your business.

LINK REQUEST: If you're being featured online ask the journalist if they can include a live link to your site. That way, readers can be on your site with one click.

Write a release

Writing a press release costs nothing but your time, yet it can generate thousands of pounds' worth of publicity. If you're emailing a press release to journalists, write the text in the body of the email and include it in an attachment, too.

Your press release should have an attention-grabbing headline, the main facts in the first sentence, and evidence and quotes from as high-profile people and companies as possible in the main body of the text. Include great quality images wherever you can to lift the piece and put a face to the brand.

You could also use a press-release distribution service to secure wider exposure. My personal favourite is ResponseSource (www.responsesource.com) but there's also PR Newswire (www.prnewswire.co.uk) and PRWeb (www.prweb.com).

If you don't get a response, follow up!

AN IMAGE SPEAKS LOUDER THAN WORDS: When a picture speaks a thousand words you can afford to talk less! Consider hiring a professional photographer to take pictures of you and your work. Maybe you can do this as a barter deal? Or pick up your own digital camera and do it yourself. Consider approaching a local college to suggest a photography student takes your images in exchange for including the end result in their portfolio. A journalist is much more likely to cover your story if you have great imagery to go with it. Use the images on your website and in promotion materials, and let your business speak for itself.

Example press release

1. Attention-grabbing headline

2. The first line is punchy and explains the what, who, why and where of the headline

3. Back up the headline and intro with more detail – facts and figures if you have them

4. Include a quote from you (or your business partner, if relevant)

5. Can you include a quote from someone else? A happy customer, industry expert or celebrity?

6. End with a call to action. Where can people go to find out more/how to download the report/which site to visit to claim a free gift, etc.?

7. Include 'Notes to Editors', with brief details on you and your company

8. Remember to include contact details – your email address and telephone number

9. Attach a relevant and interesting image

1.

2.

STARTUP SATURDAY GOES NATIONWIDE TO HELP THOUSANDS MORE GET STARTED!

Small business support company, Enterprise Nation, has announced the national expansion of its successful StartUp Saturday workshops with the 'start your own business in a day' event about to appear in new locations across the UK.

Until now, the one-day workshop that offers everything you need to know about starting a business has been delivered by Enterprise Nation founder, Emma Jones, in London. Based on feedback from small business owners around the country, we are now spreading our wings!

3.

The UK is witnessing record numbers of people starting a business with 488,000 new limited companies formed in 2011 and an all-time-high of 4.8 million small businesses operating.

StartUp Saturday was created to encourage yet more people to turn an idea into a successful venture. Enterprise Nation founder, Emma Jones, says:

"We have spent 12 months perfecting the StartUp Saturday course content and format. Budding business owners who have attended the workshop have gone on to do deals together and many of them keep in touch to offer mutual support as their business journey unfolds. Wanting to increase the number of start-ups we can help, we realised the most natural people to deliver the workshops are existing businesses owners, so the clearest route to expand was through a franchise model. We're delighted to be working with new franchisees to realise a vision of seeing StartUp Saturdays happening every week of the year and in every part of the UK!"

4.

Each StartUp Saturday session will be delivered in a fun and friendly way by talented and entrepreneurial StartUp Saturday trainers. One of the first on board is Rickie Josen, who will be hosting the workshops in Birmingham. Rickie says:

5.

"Many more people are looking to turn an idea, passion or hobby into a way of making a living and StartUp Saturday is the ideal workshop to attend to find out how to do this. In just under five hours we cover everything from business planning to sales, marketing, social media, finances, and how to create a home on the web. The workshop offers the content and confidence you need to get going and I can't wait to get started delivering it!"

6.

StartUp Saturday takes place on a monthly basis in locations around the UK, running from 10am to 3pm. The cost to attend is £35, which includes light refreshments and a *StartUp Kit*. To register for a StartUp Saturday workshop, visit **www.enterprisenation.com/saturday**

9.

MEDIA NOTES

Enterprise Nation is a small business support company offering online content, books/eBooks/Kits, events and funding to a community of over 76,000 people who are starting and growing their own venture. **www.enterprisenation.com** / **@e_nation**

7.

For media enquiries, please contact Louise Hinchen at louise@enterprisenation.com or (01234) 567 8910.

8.

Tweet, Tweet

Follow media channels, journalists and personalities on Twitter so you're the first to pick up the news and media requests:

- @BBCBreakfast
- @BBCOnthemoney
- @talktothepress
- @findaTVexpert
- @TheTimes
- @guardian
- #journorequest
- @TheoPaphitis, who runs Small Business Sunday #sbs every week between 5pm and 7.30pm where six lucky companies are re-tweeted. Full details at **tinyurl.com/smallbusinesssunday**.

And finally . . . please contact Enterprise Nation with your story. We are always profiling start-ups and small businesses on our website, in books (like this one!), in kits and in videos. Submit your story at **www.enterprisenation.com/contribute**.

KICK-STARTING WITH PR

Greg Simpson, founder and director of Press for Attention PR (**www.pressforattention.com**) gives his top 12 tips for building a successful PR campaign:

1. HAVE A 'CUNNING PLAN'

"Too many people rush into PR and marketing campaigns with no real plan. You need to consider:

- "What are the goals of the campaign?

- "How do you want to come across in terms of tone?

- "Key messages – what do you want to get across?

2. CONSIDER HOW OTHER COMPANIES GET THEIR MESSAGES ACROSS

"What tactics can you use? PR stunts, press releases, controversy, photo opportunities, comment/opinion pieces, debates, flash mobs, press trips, celebrity endorsements, competitions. There are so many ways to get noticed. Blend them to your requirements and skills.

3. RESEARCH YOUR CUSTOMER/AUDIENCE

"There is little point getting a full article page in *Dog Grooming Monthly* if you sell organic ice cream to boutique hotels! Find out who your ideal customer is and research what they read, listen to and watch. Then, really take the time to read these publications and get to know what sort of stories they publish.

4. FIND THE NEWS HOOK

"Be honest, is your story really news? Examples include: new products, new staff, new promotions, new premises, anniversaries, company expansion, financial milestones and charity efforts.

"You can also provide topical comment on a newsworthy subject. Keep an eye out for issues that affect your business or your customers. This takes practice and you need to establish credibility in your subject area first. Consider starting a blog that provides regular, lively and informed comment in your area of expertise to build your profile. I use WordPress (**www.wordpress.org**), which is free.

5. GOT A STORY?

"Got a story? Great! Now you need a simple press release for a journalist to refer to. People worry that their efforts don't sound flashy enough to warrant attention. But you aren't aiming for a Booker Prize. You're aiming for coherent and interesting *news*.

"Use 'who, what, when, how and why?' as a framework and imagine yourself as the journalist. Is this definitely of interest to their readers? Is it simple enough to understand? Does it stand up on its own?

"I would stick to a maximum of 300 words and keep the press release focused on the news angle.

6. HIT THEM BETWEEN THE EYES

"Journalists get hundreds of press releases every day. Ensure that the headline and first paragraph sum up the entire story in a nutshell. Ideally, your press release should still make sense even if an editor dropped two or three paragraphs.

"I call the journalist beforehand to outline my story. This helps iron out any creases and demonstrates that you are trying to work with them and their audience.

7. DON'T BE TEMPTED TO START HASSLING

"I very rarely 'chase' a journalist once I have sent a press release. If it is good enough, they will use it. Hassling will not push it to the top of the pile and may see it heading towards the recycle bin. Be patient and able to help if the journalist does come back and don't go on holiday the day after you have sent a story out!

8. THINK IN PICTURES

"Consider what makes you read a story when you flick through a newspaper. Headlines play their part but the impact of an interesting picture is greater still. People 'sell' stories, so ensure that anyone in your shot is clearly visible and captioned. Try to show the impact of the news – product shots are okay, but a product in the hands of a customer is better."

9. BUILD A RELATIONSHIP

"PR is not a 'them v us' war with journalists. It's a working relationship, where both parties stand to gain. They get news/insight and you get free publicity in exchange for a fresh take on things or for your role in illustrating the impact of an issue.

10. MEASURE AND EVALUATE

"How do you know if your gym regime and new diet is working? You get on the scales (peeking between your fingers). Are you getting through to the right journalists? How many stories are you sending out? How many are getting coverage? How much coverage do they get? Do your pictures and even your key messages get included? Are you being invited to comment on topical issues?

11. PUT YOUR PR HAT ON AND EXECUTE THE PLAN

"I know many small businesses that freeze when it comes to actually putting their plans into action. Schedule and commit some time every week to do something that contributes to your PR campaign.

12. A FINAL TIP

"PR agencies spend vast amounts on media monitoring software for mentions of their clients or to keep in touch with specific debates. You can do a lot of it for free. Have a play with Google Alerts (**www.google.com/alerts**)."

Appearing on TV show Be Your Own Boss *has turbo-charged Elephant Branded, a business that's helping people across the globe . . .*

CASE STUDY

James Boon never intended to be an entrepreneur or his own boss. "I simply fell into it!" he says.

Whilst at university, James spent six months building a school in South Africa. After the effort that went into the build, James was shocked to see students who came into the school were without pens or pencils, and had to do their writing on pieces of old newspaper.

"On graduation, I turned down London job offers to move to Southern China. Whilst there I travelled and again would go to schools where the kids just didn't have anything. The tipping point came when I went to Japan a couple of weeks after the 2011 tsunami hit. I moved jobs and home to Hong Kong and set up Elephant Branded with a simple idea." The idea was to ethically source bags from village cooperatives, selling them to consumers in the West and donating school kit back into the community as payment.

The original plan was to sell 50 Elephant Branded bags but when James started operating from the UK in February 2012, things took off.

"Within two weeks we had people calling us up and saying, 'How can I get involved?' We grew to have ten representatives in the UK and four overseas. The people we have met along the way have made Elephant Branded possible. From the idea of being able to donate 50 school bags we now donate thousands worldwide."

Elephant Branded has benefited from some significant profile; first by being named one of the Google Young Minds of 2012 (which resulted in a contract to supply delegate bags for Google conferences), and, more recently, in an appearance on TV show *Be Your Own Boss*.

"Since the show was aired the business has grown beyond our wildest dreams. We have had thousands of people getting in touch from all over the world. The whole experience made us question what we wanted to do with the business and on the back of it we've decided not to look for an investor because we want to keep Elephant Branded about the values it represents. Investors will (rightly) be looking for purely profit returns and that's not what we're about."

The profile and hard work put into the business has paid off in another way – in the form of a national contract with a well-known retailer:

"I received an email from John Lewis on 30 March (my birthday and a great birthday surprise!) and they have been amazing to deal with ever since. Initially we thought we might be stocked in one store. However, you can now find us in 14 of their flagship stores, including Oxford Street, as well as in their Christmas catalogue!"

James has moved out of the living room and the company now has a warehouse in Bristol and a team of five. Together the team run and manage Elephant Branded as a cooperative where everyone gets a say and a chance to shape the company's future.

Support along the way has come from Seed Education (se-ed.co.uk/edu) and StartUp Britain (www.startupbritain.co) as well as from James' business partner, Tim.

"Tim is the unsung hero of Elephant Branded. We met at university and together have been able to grow the business into what it is today. We are both quite different – Tim refers to himself as the cynic and I know I am ever the optimist and that's why it works. By both having different skill sets we each bring a lot to the table."

The team is looking to grow Elephant Branded organically and to set up new enterprises in countries such as Uganda, Sierra Leone and Columbia. The foundation of any expansion will be focused on helping local people through using local materials and leveraging local skills. In Columbia there'll be knitted products and in Uganda, bags of coffee beans – all with the elephant logo which shows the product has been ethically sourced and donated one for one.

"Elephant Branded has developed because of the people who have supported us and the people we work to support. From my friends in Hong Kong who bought the first few bags to our student reps who work on campuses around the world, and to the work by Africa Asia Venture and their volunteers who have delivered school kits. For me, what matters is that we're making a difference helping communities around the world every single day!"

- elephantbranded.com | @elephantbranded

Enter awards

Enter awards and competitions and enjoy the press coverage that goes with it. Many award schemes are free to enter and are targeted at young start-up businesses. Writing the entry will help to clarify your goals and vision, and winning will bring profile and prizes. To find out about upcoming awards across the UK, visit: www.start upbritain.co

Here are some to get you started:

- Shell LiveWIRE Grand Ideas Awards (www.shell-livewire.org/awards) – up to four awards per month of £1,000 for anyone aged 16 to 30 and looking to get an idea off the ground.

- The Pitch (www.thepitchuk.com) – enter regional heats and pitch to experienced judges for a place in the national finals and a £50,000 prize. Takes place across the UK.

- *Country Living* Magazine Kitchen Table Talent Awards (www.kitchen tabletalent.com) – if you're working on a talent or skill from the kitchen table and know it can be turned into a business, this competition is for you. Prizes include office equipment and profile in the magazine, which can be very good for sales!

- Social Enterprise Awards (www.socialenterprise.org.uk/events) – celebrates social enterprises of all ages.

- Nectar Small Business Awards (nectar.com/business-sba2012) – offers cash prizes and plenty of Nectar points!

- Startups Awards (www.startups.co.uk/startups-awards) – celebrating small businesses of all shapes and sizes.

- Smarta100 (www.smarta.com/smarta100) – an annual award to find Britain's brightest businesses with a grand prize of £10,000 in cash to the winner decided by popular vote.

- Rise To (www.riseto.co.uk) – an enterprise challenge developed by the Prelude Group (backed by The Supper Club and Red Bull) that attracts entries from teams of entrepreneurial students across the country, who each have to run a campaign championing a cause that's close to their hearts (previous winners have championed teachers, midwives and paramedics). The best teams and individuals are eligible for prizes and unique work experience shadowing successful entrepreneurs.

Host an event

Invite the press to come and meet you. This doesn't have to be an expensive affair; the secret is partnering with others who could benefit from being in front of your audience. Approach a venue and ask if you can host at no cost, in exchange for the venue receiving profile. Do the same with caterers. Then give invited guests a reason to attend – have a theme, an interesting speaker, a launch announcement, something that will grab their attention and encourage them to attend.

Make use of free online services such as Eventbrite (www.eventbrite.com) or Meetup (www.meetup.com) to send out invites and receive RSVPs.

SUCCESSFUL EVENTS IN 5 STEPS

BY EVENTBRITE

1. PLANNING = WINNING

Plan your event so you don't forget anything important. When will the event be held? When do you need to find a venue? When will tickets go on sale? When will you find sponsors by? When do you need materials delivered?

2. TAKE IT ONLINE

Create an event page on Eventbrite so you can manage sign ups and communicate with attendees in one place. You can create custom URLs, promo codes and even different ticket types, such as an early bird rate.

3. PARTNER UP

Start-ups grow and thrive off the back of collaborations. Put your event idea to contacts in the same space or at a similar stage and make it a group effort.

4. GET PEOPLE TALKING

Be remarkable! Get creative and find a USP – an unusual venue, theme or format – so people remember your event. Once that's sorted, make the most of Eventbrite's social media integration to share your event... everywhere! And don't forget to create a Twitter hashtag so attendees can spread the word for you. #Bonus!

5. STAY IN TOUCH

The event doesn't end when guests leave. Write follow up emails, newsletters, tweets, or connect on LinkedIn, and thank guests for attending. Encourage them to stay in touch and add them to your email list so they are in the loop about your next great event!

FREE CREDIT! Access a £50 credit voucher from Eventbrite at www.eventbrite.co.uk/o/template/81243

Attend events

Be seen and heard by getting out and about – a lot!

There's a wealth of events for start-ups. Most are free or low cost and offer an opportunity to learn from experts, mix with peers, and find new customers and suppliers. To see a full enterprise events listing visit www.startupbritain.co and click on Enterprise Calendar.

Across 2013 Enterprise Nation will be hosting a whole range of events designed to help you start and grow. We'd love to see you!

- StartUp Saturday (www.enterprisenation.com/saturday) – offering all you need to know to start a business in a day. Held throughout the year and across the UK.

- StartUp Workshops – a mini version of StartUp Saturday and hosted in-stores from North to South.

- SetUp Weekends – join us for a full weekend and meet Enterprise Nation authors who can get you set up online, with a new company formed and a marketing strategy in place.

- Enterprise Live! – the national Enterprise Nation event attracting hundreds of start-ups and growing businesses, with inspiring talks and activities for the kids too!

Full details for all of these can be found at the 'Events' section of **www.enterprisenation.com**.

It was attending a StartUp Saturday session that got makeup artist of six years, MaryAnn Richardson, motivated to take on a whole new venture . . .

CASE STUDY

NAME: **MaryAnn Richardson** | BUSINESS: **MaryAnn Richardson**

MaryAnn Richardson took the decision six years ago to change her career from employed office worker to self-employed make-up artist – and she doesn't regret it one bit.

"I started by taking a 10-month course in Canada which covered all areas of make-up from fashion to special effects for TV and film. Then I chose my area of speciality: I wanted to be a make-up artist for beauty advertising. I worked with photographers in the US and London and built up the portfolio that I now present to clients [you can see this on MaryAnn's site]. I am currently signed with an artists' agency in Canada who source new business and promote me through their agency."

Over the years MaryAnn has realised that, when selling yourself as an artist, your product and personality are both involved in securing new business and retaining existing customers.

"Clients choose their make-up artist based on personality as well as skill so it's very important to be personable. Clients are looking for someone to trust, whether I'm working with a bride who has never worn much make-up all her life, or a commercial client where make-up plays a part in representing their brand. Being skilled at make-up is just one area of my work; I also have to act as my own agent to sell myself (as well as being my own bookkeeper). You're a jack of all trades sometimes!"

Many of MaryAnn's clients like to know she is active in the industry and that the service on offer is on-trend. To do this MaryAnn works at fashion weeks around the world and on editorial sets for magazine publications and advertising campaigns. She also regularly contributes make-up advice for ELLE.com.

This on-trend and hardworking artist is now embarking on a new venture that will involve spending a little more time online.

"In 2013 I will be launching a blog at **www.themakeupcollaborative.com** which will be a collaboration of five make-up artists from around the world who each specialise in different areas of make-up like special effects, TV and film, fashion and beauty. I am very excited about it – and it wouldn't have kicked off without help from the StartUp Saturday workshop."

The blog will act as a community for other artists with various features such as an artist forum, profiles of up-and-coming artists and a directory for clients to find make-up artists.

"In early 2013 I will also be launching my own brush collection under my own cosmetic line makeupbymaryann. The brush set will come with a unique educational DVD on how to use each brush – perfect for make-up artists as-well as everyday beauty enthusiasts."

Working on a free blogging platform has kept start-up costs low for MaryAnn. She hasn't needed to raise investment. It's given her more time to focus on the promotion of the blog and new brush line.

"I'll be making sure the blog becomes a useful source of information for artists and looking into the potential growth of the brushes by working with individual charities for special edition brushes. It is going to be a very exciting year!"

- www.maryannrichardson.com

In terms of events there's also . . .

- Global Entrepreneurship Week (November each year) | www.gew.org.uk
- NACUE events at universities and colleges | nacue.com
- StartUp Weekend: hosted in locations across the UK | www.startupweekend.org
- StartUp Britain Industry Weeks, national tour, and StartUp Day | www.startupbritain.co

Jump On Board!

Rolling into its third year in 2013, the national StartUp Britain Tour sees a bright and buzzing bus travel to universities and colleges with entrepreneurs and experts on board. Register to receive the StartUp Britain e-news (**www.startupbritain.co**) and you'll be first to hear about bus tour dates and locations.

Join a society, group or club

Signing up to an enterprise society, a local business club or network is good for business (and your social life). Check out these national business and society networks to find your natural fit:

- Enterprise Nation – friendly community of over 75,000 business owners who benefit from daily content with premium members receiving profile, free eBooks, and discounts on events. www.enterprisenation.com

- 4Networking – national network of business breakfast groups. www.4networking.biz

- Business Scene – hosts regional and national networking events as well as an online directory of over 10,000 events across the UK. www.business-scene.com

- Jelly – casual gatherings of co-workers, with events held in people's homes, the local coffee shop or co-working spaces. The idea is that you meet in relaxed surroundings and creative ideas are stimulated by the experience. www.workatjelly.com

- NACUE – the national organisation that supports and represents student-led enterprise societies and young entrepreneurs in universities and colleges across the UK. www.nacue.com

- The Gazelle Group – 20-plus further education colleges focused on developing entrepreneurial students and environments. www.thegazellegroup.com

- School for Startups – headed by serial entrepreneur Doug Richard, School for Startups travels the UK hosting events for anyone considering starting a business. www.schoolforstartups.co.uk

- Young Entrepreneur Society – founded by young entrepreneur Carly Ward, this is a network that offers education and monthly events to budding business owners. www.youngentrepreneursociety.org.uk

- Intuit 100Up – apply to be part of this group of 100 StartUps and receive access to finance bootcamps and mentoring via a partnership with NACUE. nacue.com/2012/03/introducing-intuit-100up

- Professional Contractors Group (PCG) – if contracting is the life for you, check out the free resources and events hosted by PCG. www.pcg.org.uk

- Virgin Media Pioneers – create a profile and connect with others, plus have the opportunity to pitch to Sir Richard Branson himself via this vibrant network of young entrepreneurs. www.virginmediapioneers.com

As your business grows, why not offer to go and speak to those younger than you who dream of following in your footsteps? Do so by linking up with:

- Peter Jones Enterprise Academy – started by *Dragons' Den* entrepreneur Peter Jones, the academy offers a full-time educational course and qualification in enterprise and entrepreneurship for 16–19 year olds. www.pjea.org.uk

- Young Enterprise – a charity that helps 250,000 young people every year to learn more about business. www.young-enterprise.org.uk

- School Speakers – started by entrepreneur and *Apprentice* TV star Claire Young, this organisation matches enterprising and inspiring speakers with schools. www.schoolspeakers.co.uk

- Inspiring the Future – deliver an enterprising talk at a local school and pass on lessons learned. www.inspiringthefuture.org

BECOME A STARTUP LOCAL CHAMPION: Raise your profile and the likelihood of being approached for talks and coverage in national campaigns by becoming a StartUp Britain Local Champion. As a Local Champ, you'll be the face of StartUp Britain in your area and have opportunities to get involved in projects like High Street StartUp and StartUp Spaces. It's a route to making connections and, best of all, encouraging even more people to become their own boss.

Attend trade shows

Promote your brand by attending the shows your customers attend. Research the best shows by reading industry magazines and visiting online forums where people in your sector are talking.

Trade show tactics

Before the event

Negotiate a good deal – if you're prepared to wait it out, the best deals on stands can be had days before the event is starting. The closer the date, the better the price you'll negotiate as the sales team hurry to get a full house.

Tell people you're going – circulate news that you'll be at the event through online networks (giving your location or stand number) and issue a press release if you're doing something newsworthy at the event, maybe launching a new product, having a guest appearance, running a competition, etc.

At the event

Be clear on the offer – determine what you are selling at the show and let this be consistent across show materials; from pop-up stands to flyers. Be creative with the stand to keep costs low. Pop-up banners can be bought for £45 each from companies like Demonprint (www.demonprint.co.uk). Consider offering a supply of mouth-watering refreshments and branded accessories like pens, bags and t-shirts which can be ordered from companies like Vistaprint (www.vistaprint.co.uk).

- Collect data – find ways to collect attendees' names and details. Offer a prize in exchange for business cards or take details in exchange for a follow-up information pack or offer. Some events also offer the facility to scan the details from the delegates' badges (for a fee).

- Take friends/family – invite a supportive team. If you're busy talking to a potential customer, you'll want others on the stand who can be doing the same. If there's time, get to know the exhibitors around you.

- Be prepared – wear comfortable shoes, bring some spare clothes and pack your lunch; if you're busy there may not be time to spend buying food and drink!

After the event

- Follow-up – within a couple of days of returning from the show, contact the people who expressed interest so that interest can be turned into sales.

- Plan ahead – if the show delivered a good return, contact the organisers and ask to be considered for a speaking slot or higher profile at the next event, and confirm your willingness to be a case study testimonial story in any post-show promotion.

Become an expert

If you have a special set of knowledge or experience, set yourself up as an expert in your field and the media will come knocking on your door. Here are eight ways in which you can promote your expertise.

1. Publish a book

Become a published author on your special topic. Utilise the book as a business development tool, taking copies to events, and offering free and downloadable versions to potential customers. Being an author lends you credibility and gives customers information and insight. Get in touch with publishers and agents via *The Writer's & Artist's Yearbook*, or self-publish:

- Blurb | www.blurb.com
- Lulu | www.lulu.com
- Ubyu | www.ubyubooks.com

2. Present yourself

Put yourself forward to speak at events (consider asking for a fee and/or costs to be covered) or suggest being a satellite speaker, where you are beamed in via video link-up, so saving the effort and expense of travel. Invite customers and prospects and make the presentation openly available via SlideShare or Prezi.

- SlideShare | www.slideshare.com
- Prezi | www.prezi.com

3. Host a webinar

Share your expertise or demonstrate a process by hosting a webinar or visual presentation where a live audience can see you and interact. Achieve this via platforms such as GoToMeeting, GoToWebinar and WebEx, and remember to host it at a time that suits your target audience.

- GoToMeeting | www.gotomeeting.com
- GoToWebinar | www.gotomeeting.com/webinar
- WebEx | www.webex.co.uk

4. Produce a film

Maybe the word 'film' is a little ambitious but why not create your own video content and have a sponsored series of guides (or other content) that can be uploaded to video sharing sites such as YouTube, Vimeo and eHow?

- YouTube | www.youtube.com
- Vimeo | www.vimeo.com
- eHow | www.ehow.co.uk

5. Broadcast a podcast

For customers who like to listen to what you have to say at a time that suits them, upload a podcast with top tips, interviews and your thoughts of the day. Make it available on your site, iTunes and Podcast Alley to be sure of a wide audience. Follow the advice below from podcast producer San Sharma on how to record a podcast on a Skype call.

- Submit a podcast to the iTunes store | www.apple.com/itunes/podcasts

- Podcast Alley | www.podcastalley.com

YOU CAN PRODUCE A PODCAST interview using Skype, Pamela Call Recorder, and a little editing know-how. San Sharma shows how it's done, in five simple steps:

1. "Sign up for a free Skype account (www.skype.com) and download the Skype software.

2. "If you're using a Windows machine, download Pamela Call Recorder (www.pamela.biz), which lets you record your Skype calls. If you're on a Mac, you can download Call Recorder for Skype (www.ecamm.com). Both have free trial versions, but only cost around £13 when that's expired.

3. "Call up your interviewee using Skype. If they're a Skype user, too, that will be a free call but if they're on a fixed or mobile line, you'll need to get some Skype Credit (bit.ly/epymNm).

4. "Once you've made a connection and agreed with the interviewee the format of the conversation, hit the record button on your call recorder software and you're off!

5. "Edit using Audacity (audacity.sourceforge.net), which is free for Windows and Macs, or with GarageBand (www.apple.com/garageband), which comes with most Macs (you can also buy it as part of the iLife package).

"The easiest way to share your recording is by uploading it to AudioBoo (www.audioboo.com), which lets people listen to it on the web, embedded on your website or via iTunes or a mobile phone."

6. Deliver training

Whether your skill is in embroidering handmade shoes or developing stylish websites, your knowledge could be shared with others. Rather than seeing this as surrendering intelligence to potential competitors, offer instruction you're comfortable with that will create fans and followers who will learn from you, buy from you and, critically, encourage others to do the same. Check out platforms GoToTraining, WebEx and Blackboard, encourage contacts to sign up and then after the demonstration you have a chance to follow up with a group of new contacts.

- GoToTraining | www.gotomeeting.com/fec/training/online_training
- WebEx WebTraining | www.webex.co.uk
- Blackboard | www.blackboard.com

7. Develop an app

Take your content and make an iPhone app. Turn to browser-based platforms such as Appmakr; "AppMakr can be used by anyone with existing content and fans or customers to reach; bloggers/writers, business owners, website owners . . . ".

You can either set a list price to make sales via the App Store or make it available free of charge.

- AppMakr | www.appmakr.com

8. Form groups

Encourage others to discuss, debate and contribute to your content by forming groups utilising social media platforms such as Facebook, LinkedIn and Ning. Bonding interested people to each other will bond them ever closer to you, the content creator and group host.

- Facebook | www.facebook.com
- LinkedIn | www.linkedin.com
- Ning | www.ning.com

> **BE EVERYWHERE**: Keep in touch with existing customers via a newsletter and reach out to the new by making regular appearances at events, on other people's websites and blogs, in newspapers and magazines, and on radio and TV. Write to the magazines and radio stations that ask people to send in their story. It's a free way to get coverage. The more you're covered, the more you'll be invited to speak and comment, and before you know it, you'll be everywhere!

Price point

These options will raise your profile but you can also generate revenue from them. Your options are:

- make your content and knowledge available at no charge to customers, to build your reputation as the go-to person and place for a particular product or service

- charge for access/downloads/viewing and turn your micropublishing activity into a revenue stream in its own right.

This is something you can assess over time. Start with a mix of charged-for and free content, ensure you're providing good value and incentives for your community to remain interested and engaged, and the options to introduce charged-for content will increase.

Magdalena Marsden has taken her part-time venture and turned it into a year-round business, selling handmade crafts and food and running a bread-making course . . .

CASE STUDY

NAME: **Magdalena Marsden** | BUSINESS: **Cocoa & Heart**

Ever since early childhood Magdalena Marsden has been creative. From an early age she was always making something, whether a piece of jewellery or a new skirt. At the same time she also developed a talent for baking and cooking; over the years she became well-known amongst friends and family for her delicious chocolate truffles! And in 2011, after working on the craft side of her interests in her spare time, she was finally able to turn this creativity into a full-time living.

"For the last 12 years I would do just one craft fair a year before Christmas and sell my products. I would take annual leave from my paid job a week before the fair and just enjoy the time making things. Then work started to become difficult, with lots of office politics going on. I finally decided to leave to prevent complete exhaustion and burnout.

I didn't want to jump straight into another job, so I thought that perhaps the time had come to follow my dream and set up my own business."

Cocoa & Heart was launched in 2011 and is all about handmade living, with the main part of the business focused on artisan baking and chocolate-making, and a secondary line in fabric decorations and crafts.

"I was fortunate in that my customers, who had only seen me once a year, were very supportive and quickly formed a solid customer base. To reach out further I promoted my business through social media, local and regional craft fairs, my own website, and other websites that are relevant to my business."

Being passionate about good bread – and having baked her own for a decade – Magdalena later turned her kitchen into a workspace and expanded the business through offering a bread-making course.

"My courses have quickly become popular and everyone who comes is amazed what they can make with just a few ingredients. I wanted to offer a homely environment and friendly feel on the courses. The kitchen takes up to four people and the small group and individual attention means every student gets as much out of the day as possible. And of course I serve my own bread with lunch, and everyone is welcomed with freshly baked cake and coffee!"

The skills picked up during her career helped Magdalena get started in business but she also attended workshops at a local centre, with the one-to-one support sessions proving particularly valuable.

"I'm used to finding my own information, so I've found the internet really useful for business advice and support – in particular various craft and business forums and (of course) Enterprise Nation!"

Magdalena feels her first business year was spent working out what works and what does not. The following one will be all about improving on that.

"I want to expand my range of baking courses and do regular markets with my chocolates to become known more locally. At the back of my mind I do have plans for a shop/coffee place/workshop hub, but that's probably still in the distant future."

Magdalena is helped in her ambitions by a supportive husband who attends fairs and acts as a sounding board for new ideas.

"He is my rock and makes me laugh when he comes home from his job and wants to know how my day was, because as he says, 'There is always something interesting happening in your "work"!' "

- www.cocoaandheart.co.uk | @cocoaandheart

Embrace social media

Thanks to social media, there have never been so many tools to promote our businesses free of charge. According to research company Nielsen, the world now spends over 110 billion minutes on social networks and blogs per month. That's 22% of all time online, or one in every four and a half minutes. Embrace this and your business will become known. Here are the key tools to use and, crucially, how best to use them.

Facebook

Facebook has over 1 billion users worldwide, so if you need to be where your customers are, there's a good chance some of them will be there!

You can list on Facebook for free and/or advertise on the site and select target audience based on location, sex, age and interests. As an advertiser, you control how much you want to spend and set a daily budget. The minimum budget is US $1.00 (63p) a day. After designing your ad(s), decide for how long you want the campaign to run and whether you want to be charged for the number of clicks you receive (CPC – charge per click) or the number of times your ad is displayed. Visit www.facebook.com, create an account, invite friends and contacts to join your group and get promoting.

Download the free eBook *Boost your Business on Facebook* at www.enterprise nation.com/facebook-book-offer.

- **Cost**: free (ads are charged-for)

Twitter

Visit www.twitter.com, create an account, follow friends and contacts (and their followers) and get tweeting.

- **Cost**: free

HOW TO BE A SUCCESS ON TWITTER

Twitter expert Mark Shaw (**@markshaw**) shares his four top tips that will have you tweeting like a pro:

1. **"BE COMMITTED**. Add a good photo, perhaps a bespoke background, your URL and an interesting bio. Try and differentiate yourself and make sure the bio contains keywords so that others can find you.

2. **"BE CONSISTENT**. Show up each day and tweet, even if time is short. It's more important to do a small amount each day than lots one day and then nothing for a week or so.

3. **"BE INTERESTING**. Try and tweet three types of messages: social chit-chat; the sharing of resources, links, tools, info, ideas and opinions; and tweets that answer questions which demonstrate your knowledge. Aim for a good balance.

4. **"BE INTERESTED**. Engage with others by answering questions and joining in. Find conversations to enter into via **search.twitter.com** and retweet (RT) other people's messages if they are of interest to you and your followers. It's not about selling things but it is all about building your brand and credibility."

Flickr

Join **www.flickr.com** and promote yourself visually by uploading photos of you and your products or service, and maybe even a few shots of happy customers. The site also carries video clips so you can show:

- events you host, speak at, or attend
- products you make (the finished product) as well as images of the production process
- happy customers wearing/using/enjoying your products and services
- your workspace
- your family (if you – and they – feel comfortable showing your personal side).

You can also easily pull the photos into your blog and social media pages.

- **Cost**: free (option to upgrade to a pro account which is a paid-for package)

LinkedIn

Referring to itself as "the world's largest professional network", LinkedIn has over 100 million members in 200-plus countries. Visit **www.linkedin.com**, create an account and start connecting with contacts and finding new ones. Form LinkedIn groups around your specialist subject; or, if you are a professional selling creative services, check out the Creative Portfolio Display application (**linkd.in/deDVX1**), which aims to "empower creative professionals by creating a one-stop solution for maintaining their work portfolio and broadcasting it to millions".

- **Cost**: free (option to upgrade to a business account, which is a paid-for package)

YouTube

YouTube is the world's most popular online video community, with 24 hours of video uploaded every minute. Start your own business channel for free, and upload videos profiling you and your work.

Create an account (**www.youtube.com/create_account**), start a channel (advice via YouTube video!), and start broadcasting to the world. You can give each of your videos a name and assign keywords to it to help with searching, plus you can have a short description of your company on your profile page. Again, these clips are very easy to add to your website, and they help keep the content fresh and interesting.

- **Cost**: free

Pinterest

Pinterest is a virtual pinboard that lets users organise and share the beautiful things they find on the web. Big brands and small businesses have taken to Pinterest to pin pictures of their products to virtual 'pinboards'. More powerfully, customers are pinning their favourite products – and doing some of the marketing work for them!

The site has just over 2 million daily active users. Head to **tinyurl.com/ENPinterest** to view other Pinteresting facts and figures.

- **Cost:** free

TOTAL BUDGET REQUIRED FOR ONLINE PROMOTION: £0

Measure the results

Time to measure what's working and what's not. Measure media and press mentions through signing up to Google Alerts – and you'll be pleased to know there's a whole host of tools that are free to use and will show real-time results for what's working on your site.

Google Analytics offers intelligence on your website traffic and marketing effectiveness: www.google.com/analytics

There are other analytics options:

- Alexa – web traffic metrics, site demographics and top URL listings: www.alexa.com

- Clicky – monitors and analyses your site traffic in real time: www.getclicky.com

- Opentracker – gather and analyse web stats and monitor online visitors: www.opentracker.net

- StatCounter – an invisible web tracker and hit counter that offers data in real time: www.statcounter.com

- Marketing Grader – generates a free marketing report that compares your site with a competitor's: www.websitegrader.com

Hopefully what you will see is an upward curve of visitors and time spent on the site.

If you're selling anything, then hopefully this means more sales. If your site is the business, this means you're in a strong position to attract advertisers and begin doing affiliate deals.

MONKEYING AROUND: Run a poll with, for example, Wufoo (www.wufoo.com) or Survey Monkey (www.surveymonkey.com). Both are free to use, then publish the results via a press release and online. The media loves good polls!

Look out, in particular, for the sources of your traffic (which are your highest referring sites) and your most popular pages. You can see days where your site receives spikes in visitor levels (and track this back to marketing) and measure if visitors are spending longer periods on the site and which times are popular, e.g. weekends, evenings, lunchtimes, etc.

Use the following template to ensure you're making the most of all your marketing opportunities.

Template 7: Marketing and Promotion

Media

Press (local and national)

List relevant names and journalists

Radio

List programmes on which you'd like to appear

Television

List programmes on which you'd like to appear

Magazines

List target titles

Online

List target sites

Other

Events

List events to attend; networking and trade. What about hosting your own event, too?

Awards

List awards relevant to your business and their dates of entry

Your social network

Plan of action for engaging with major social networks on ongoing basis

III. GROW

With marketing and sales underway, you are getting known and making money. Now it's time to grow your profits by outsourcing, keeping the business in balance, staying on top of cash flow and getting some good support.

66 Write your own rules –
whilst you shouldn't
ignore advice from other
successful entrepreneurs,
don't be a slave to their
methods. You know your
business best and can
navigate your own way. 99

– Jess Butcher,
founder, Blippar

13. ATTRACT CUSTOMERS BACK

You are making sales via your site and developing a strong community of fans and followers. Give visitors and customers a reason to return with content that is regularly updated.

If you have a blog, try to post regularly, and if you're selling, keep the product range updated. Give your site some TLC each day, as fresh content will attract visitors who want to see what's new and will also appeal to the trawling web spiders who determine search engine results.

User-generated content

Encourage your site visitors to get to know each other through a forum or comment boxes. Before you know it, a sense of community will develop and visitors will log on each day to find out who's saying what and what's happening with whom.

Exclusive offers

Extend offers to your existing customers, readers or members that will tempt them back. This offer could be conditional on customers referring a friend: that way your customer returns to the site with others in tow. Add to this with a badge of honour; design an icon that visitors can display on their own site to show their affiliation with you.

Guest appearances

Invite special guests to appear on your site via guest blog posts, hosting a webchat or a featured interview.

Keep in touch

Communicate all these good and sticky things to your users through a regular e-newsletter powered by sites such as MailChimp (**www.mailchimp.com**), Constant Contact (**www.constantcontact.com**) or AWeber Communications (**www.aweber.com**).

Email marketing: keep it clean, keep it simple, keep it relevant

Email marketing works best when it is targeted. This means keeping your lists clean and organising them according to previous customer contact. A well-segmented list means you can send more frequent campaigns, ensuring a steady flow of business, without worrying about clogging up inboxes. Keep your email designs clean and simple – making it easier for your customer to make informed buying decisions in a snap.

14. FOCUS ON WHAT YOU DO BEST AND OUTSOURCE THE REST

The business is growing, time is your most precious resource and you are in need of help. The quickest and most affordable place to get it is from other companies with whom you can partner to get projects done, as well as from expert advisors and mentors who will offer advice on how the business can continue to grow.

With outsourcing you can free yourself up to dedicate your attention to sales, strategy or whatever the business activity is that you do best. My advice to all businesses is always: *focus on what you do best and outsource the rest.*

What can be outsourced and to whom?

Admin

Hire a VA (virtual assistant) to do the admin tasks you don't want or don't have the time to do:

- International Association of Virtual Assistants | www.iava.co.uk
- Society of Virtual Assistants | www.societyofvirtualassistants.co.uk
- VA Success Group | www.vasuccessgroup.co.uk
- Virtual Assistant Coaching & Training Company | www.vact.co.uk
- Virtual Assistant Forums | www.virtualassistantforums.com

Accounts

Unless you are in the accountancy business, this is almost a must to be outsourced. Monthly payroll, accounts, VAT returns and corporate tax returns all take time and it's time you can't afford or simply don't have. A cost/benefit analysis is likely to show that it's cheaper to outsource to a qualified accountant. Ask around for recommendations of accountants in your area who deliver a quality service at a competitive cost and are registered with the Institute of Chartered Accountants for England and Wales.

For online accounting and invoicing that makes life easier for you and your accountant, check out:

- FreeAgent | www.freeagent.com
- KashFlow | www.kashflow.co.uk
- QuickBooks | www.quickbooks.co.uk

IN THE KIT

Access free trials with FreeAgent and Intuit.

PR, marketing and design

Outsource your PR to a specialist who can be pitching and promoting the business whilst you're at work. Find skilled professionals on directory sites such as Enterprise Nation (www.enterprisenation.com), oDesk (www.odesk.com) and PeoplePerHour (www.peopleperhour.com).

Sales

Hire a sales expert to make calls, set up appointments and attend trade shows. Find these professionals online, contact telemarketing companies that offer outbound sales calls as a service, or look at sales specialists such as Winning Sales (www.winningsales.co.uk).

Customer service

Looking after customers is vital, but even that can be outsourced. Get Satisfaction's tagline is "people-powered customer service" – it provides a web-hosted platform, much like a forum, where customers can ask questions, suggest improvements, report a problem or give praise. It can save you time and money by having the power of the crowd take care of customer questions!

- Get Satisfaction | www.getsatisfaction.com

IT

Spending too many hours trying to fix a single IT problem? Outsource the hassle and save your time, money and blood pressure. Find IT professionals online or contact IT support teams connected to the large retailers.

- Geeks-on-Wheels | www.geeks-on-wheels.com
- Knowhow | www.knowhow.com
- Geek Squad | www.geeksquad.co.uk

Steps to successful outsourcing

Do the groundwork

Spend some time working on the task yourself so you've built foundations before handing it over to someone else. For example, if you outsource sales then have a ready-made contacts list and some open doors that the specialist can build on, rather than starting from scratch. This will make it more cost-effective for you and means that they hit the ground running.

Be clear on the brief

Having spent some time doing the task yourself, you will have a clear idea of the brief. Back to the example of outsourcing sales, if you've spent 6–12 months sourcing leads and making contacts, you'll have a much clearer idea of the type of work the specialist should do.

The clearer the brief, the better the results.

Take your time

And take references. Spend time evaluating the specialists in the market and, if you can, talk to their existing clients. Do they have the industry experience you're after?

Will they represent your brand in a professional manner? Have they delivered a good job for other clients? When an outsourced arrangement works well, the partner becomes part of your team – so choose them as carefully as you would choose an employee.

Let go!

Outsourcing means having to let go a little. Someone else becomes accountable for these results. Embrace this rather than resist it. As the business owner you remain in ultimate control but the expert will need their own space in which to flourish. Outsourcing can save you time and help make you money. Finding the right partner, on the right terms, will make you feel like a new and liberated person.

IN THE KIT

Get $50 in oDesk Credits to hire online contractors and $200 worth of recruiting services, with experienced oDesk recruiters helping you find the perfect contractor for your first job.

Form teams

Once you've chosen your outsourced partner(s), it's important to keep in regular contact and work together as a team. There are a number of online project management and collaboration tools to help you stay on top of projects and in control of the company.

- Basecamp (**www.basecamp.com**) is the project management tool we rely on at Enterprise Nation. This is a top-class product that allows you to create projects, invite people to view them, upload files and make comments. It's effective online project management that can be accessed from anywhere.

- Share documents via Google Docs (**docs.google.com**). You can edit on the move, choose who accesses documents and share changes in real time.

- Huddle (**www.huddle.com**) offers simple and secure online workspaces. Huddle is hosted, so there's no software to download and it's free to get started.

Solutions to enable group-talk

- GoToMeeting | www.gotomeeting.com

Work with anyone, anywhere with this easy to use online meeting tool.

- Ketchup | www.useketchup.com

Share and record meeting notes.

- Powwownow | www.powwownow.co.uk

Free conference calling at 'open access' level. Priced packages available.

- OmniJoin | webconferencing.brother.co.uk

Hold secure and reliable meetings in high definition video and high quality VoIP (Voice over IP) audio with up to 50 people.

CASE STUDY

NAME: **Matthew Ogston** | BUSINESS: **JobPage**

Matthew Ogston's business is a social network designed to help people find their perfect job. JobPage works by connecting job seekers with other job seekers in the search for freelance, permanent, full-time and job-share work, or even apprenticeships.

Matthew believes in focusing what you do best and outsourcing work to other professionals. It's a philosophy he follows with help from the world's largest online workplace, **oDesk.com**.

"I heard about oDesk from an ex-colleague who had built up a successful freelance web-development company using oDesk contractors whilst still maintaining his full-time job. He was managing the contractors in his lunchtime and evenings, successfully using the tools provided by oDesk. He was earning a very good extra income. I was instantly hooked and opened my oDesk account the same day."

The first contractors Matthew hired were web developers. Since then he has continuously had at least one oDesk developer on staff – managed entirely via **oDesk.com** and the oDesk iPhone app.

"The JobPage team is made up of oDesk contractors, personally hired freelancers, and the company founders. Our small team is spread out across the UK, Poland, Bulgaria, Italy and India. Next year we plan to expanding the team further, bringing on new skills, from new locations."

To find the highest-rated contractors in each of the areas where the business needed resources, Matthew used the oDesk oConomy league tables. Since then, relationships have developed and JobPage has found itself still working, two years on, with a number of the contractors initially found via the site.

"Most of our contractors are based in Europe so we don't have too many challenges with timezones. Our team is very flexible when it comes to start and end times for each working day as no two days are the same. We communicate using PivotalTracker for development tasks, Asana for project management, SVN for code management, Google Docs, Skype and email."

Matthew gives credit to oDesk for having helped his business grow in a cost-effective way. With hourly rates in non-UK countries set at competitive levels, using oDesk contractors offers good value, without any compromise on quality as there's a large community of world-class professionals and experts ready to be hired via oDesk.

With plans for a new website in 2013, and new revenue streams too, Matthew and his oDesk team are looking forward to an exciting year of growth ahead.

- **jobpage.com** | @job_page

Form partnerships

If relationships develop, you may decide to form a partnership. Consider writing a partnership agreement as your pre-nup in business. At the outset of a relationship, all is good and you're excited about the potential, but it's best to be safe; have the terms written and agreed so that all parties are clear on expectations.

The following should not be taken as concrete legal advice, more of a guideline on how to draw up an agreement.

Scope of agreement

What is your partnership working to achieve? For example, "This agreement is made between Company A and Company B. The agreement is related to the generation of online advertising revenues/hosting of an event/development of a new product."

Respective responsibilities

Set out the expectations on who does what. For example, Company A will be responsible for promotion and business development and Company B will take on technical development and client care. Also include a note of how you'll keep each other briefed, maybe through the use of an online project management tool.

Finances

What will be the split in revenue, and is this before or after costs? And who owns the intellectual property of the product/service/activity? Consider including a clause that states the agreement will be reviewed in six months so that both parties can check on progress and have the right to cease the agreement if it hasn't gone as planned.

Be fair

Agreements where both parties feel that they're receiving their fair share are likely to be longer-lasting than those when one party feels embittered. Talk about this before writing and concluding the agreement. Make sure there's no resentment or sense of being exploited on either side.

Sign it!

After making the effort to produce an agreement, be sure to sign it! And then store it so that you can access it easily if the need arises.

When writing the clauses in your agreement, think about all the things that could go wrong and safeguard against them. It's a practical exercise and won't harm your newly formed business relationship but will get it off on a firm footing. If you're looking for a template agreement, check out sites such as **www.clickdocs.co.uk**.

BUSINESS OWNER PLUS ONE: When the business is at a stage to take on its first new employee, visit the 'Growing your business' section of the GOV.UK site (**www.gov.uk/growing-your-business/hire-and-train-staff**), which offers details on how to employ and your obligations as an employer over time.

15. KEEP THE BUSINESS IN BALANCE

As the business continues to grow, you will want to maintain momentum and grow at a comfortable pace. Achieve this by following what I call 'the golden triangle', which will keep you and the business in balance. This requires spending roughly a third of your time on three key things:

1. Customer care

Look after your customers by delivering a quality product or service, on time and within budget. And remember . . . the customer is always right!

I ask clients for feedback so that I can keep a check on what they're thinking and changes they'd like to see. It's good to know some personal details about your customers, too. (Maybe their birthday, their favourite hobby.) As you gather these details, make a quick note so you can send a birthday card on the right date, etc. Don't go overboard, but showing that you care certainly won't harm your relationship.

Offer customers good service, regular communication and an innovative line of products and services. It will stand you in good stead.

2. New business

Taking care of customers means taking care of sales. Why? Because it costs less to win business from existing customers than it does to find new ones. If customers are happy, they'll say good things about you to new and potential customers. This is called word-of-mouth marketing and achieving it is every business owner's dream!

Secure new clients through marketing, encouraging recommendations, and direct-sales calls and pitches.

3. Admin

Not as enjoyable as the first two, but it still has to be done. Keep the books in order by raising invoices in good time, being on top of cash flow, and filing tax returns and company documents on time and in order. In short, keep the finances in check and the books up-to-date.

Cash is king

In Chapter 9 we looked at the topic of straightforward finance and how to plan income and outgoings.

Keep an eye on the accounts so you can see how much money is in the bank, how much is owed and whether this covers your outgoings.

This is a vital part of running your business and something you will need to keep close tabs on especially at the start. Monitor this using your accounts software and online banking. It's a very well-worn phrase in business, but cash is most definitely king.

Getting paid and paying others

A key part in managing your cash flow is making sure you get paid and get paid promptly. How you get paid will depend quite a lot on the type of business you have and whether you are selling direct to customers or to other businesses. If selling directly, you will mostly be paid immediately. If you are dealing with other businesses, the chances are most will expect to pay on invoice (more on this below) and will expect a credit period in which to pay. Be prepared to offer credit terms, but be careful about how long you give, how much credit you'll allow and who you offer this to.

If you need to buy in products or services from others as part of your business it's always worth seeing if you too can arrange credit terms with suppliers. This should help you balance payments in and out. This isn't always easy at the start and you may have to pay upfront to begin with, but it is something to ask for. Having built up a good relationship with your supplier it should be a natural next step.

Invoices

Be on time with invoicing and keep a record of amounts outstanding. I have a simple spreadsheet with five columns labelled 'client', 'invoice amount', 'invoice number', 'date submitted' and 'date paid'.

- Your invoices should be a simple document with basic details. The less cause for question on the invoice, the faster it will be paid.

- Always find out in advance who should be named on the invoice, where it should be sent and whether you need to include any sort of order reference number. When dealing with large companies in particular, this sort of thing can make a big difference to how quickly you get paid.

- Settle invoices as promptly as you can. Your suppliers should be grateful and repay you with good service.

See the next page for an example invoice.

Hopefully your clients and customers will always pay promptly, but occasionally you might need to remind them. Do this politely and clearly. It's often sensible to send a monthly statement to a client detailing any outstanding invoices, and usually that's enough to spur them into action.

You can balance the budget with a piece of accounting software. See 'Accounts' earlier for details of options, and don't forget to have a look at the offers available in this kit.

Receipts

Keep business-related receipts in a place where they're easy to find. I have a big wicker box that I use as a collecting place for receipts. It's helpful that they're all in one place when it's time to do the VAT return.

Track your time with time-tracking software

- Cashboard | www.getcashboard.com

- Four Four Time | www.fourfourtime.co.uk

- TraxTime | www.spudcity.com/traxtime

SAMPLE INVOICE

1. Name of your contact

2. The date

3. An address to which the cheque shall be sent or bank details for accounts in which monies should be deposited

4. Company registration and VAT number (if applicable)

5. Invoice number and client's purchase order (PO) number

6. Payment terms (e.g. payable within 30 days of receipt), and by cheque, transfer, etc.

7. A brief product description or summary of services

8. Amount owing (inclusive or exclusive of VAT, depending on whether you're registered).

I think it's good practice to include a cover note, too, that confirms what's being invoiced and thanks the client for their custom.

Invoice

1.

YOUR SMALL BUSINESS

Attention: Joe Smith
Managing Director
A. N. Other Small Business
321 First Street
Anytown, County AB1 2CD
Date 29/01/2012 **2.**

3.
Your small business address
123 Second Street
Anothertown, County AB2 3CD
T 01234 567 8910
F 01234 567 8911
you@youremailaddress.com
http://www.yourwebsite.com/

4.
Your company registration
VAT no. 12345678910

PROJECT TITLE: A. N. Other Small Business website
PROJECT DESCRIPTION: Redesign of business website **5.**
INVOICE NUMBER: 01
TERMS: 30 days **6.**

8.

7.

Description	Amount owed
Graphic design	£1,500.00
Programming	£2,000.00
Hosting	£500.00
Total	**£4,000.00**

Please make cheque payable to Your Name and deliver to the
address printed on this invoice.

Sincerely yours,

Your Name

16. SUPPORT

All of the success stories in this kit have spoken of the valuable support received from friends, family, advisors and experienced entrepreneurs.

Ask questions at every opportunity and build a support network. Here's where to look for people who are happy to help.

Peers

Who better to turn to than those going through the same experience as you? Visit the sites below and join their active communities of business owners.

- Enterprise Nation | www.enterprisenation.com
- Business Zone | www.businesszone.co.uk
- Start Up Donut | www.startupdonut.co.uk
- Smarta | www.smarta.com
- Startups | startups.co.uk
- Fresh Business Thinking | www.freshbusinessthinking.com
- School for Startups | www.schoolforstartups.co.uk

Mentors

Find a mentor through making a direct approach to experts, professionals and business owners you admire and respect. Or source one via government website Mentorsme.co.uk.

And don't restrict yourself to one mentor! I have learnt from many people as my businesses have passed through different stages of development. My approach was to get in touch with the person I felt best placed to have the answer, take on board their views, consider my options, and then act.

In my view, the ideal mentor is someone who possesses four things:

1. experience of your industry/sector
2. the ability to listen
3. the technical skills to advise
4. a willingness to make introductions to useful contacts.

If you can find these in one person, you are very fortunate indeed.

One of the finest things a mentor can do is allow you to talk. By doing so, you often work out the answer. Sometimes you just need an experienced sounding board.

Business advisors

Consider approaching your local enterprise agency, university/college society, chamber of commerce or the Prince's Trust for additional support.

- National Enterprise Network (**www.nationalenterprisenetwork.org**) offers links to local business support agencies in your area.
- NACUE (**www.nacue.org**) represents enterprise societies in universities and colleges that could be your first port of call.
- In 2011, the Prince's Trust (**tinyurl.com/princestrustenterprise**) helped almost 13,000 young people through its Enterprise Programme.
- Local Enterprise Partnerships (**www.bis.gov.uk/policies/economic-development/leps**) have been set up to encourage enterprise and will be interested in hearing any success story.
- British Chambers of Commerce (**www.britishchambers.org.uk**) offer specific services relating to export. Some have Junior Chambers for younger members.

In starting her business, Skye Robertson has not been shy in approaching people and organisations set up to support budding entrepreneurs. What she's discovered is, if you seek – you will find . . .

CASE STUDY

Skye Robertson grew up in a small town with access to great local produce, breads and jams. On leaving home, Skye then found it difficult to be surrounded by supermarkets where local or artisan produce was just not on offer. This young and entrepreneurial lady realised there was a gap in the market to bring great artisan foods, prepared by small food businesses, to the wider public.

"With busy schedules and long commutes it isn't always easy for us to pop down to the farmers' market and do our shopping like many of us would like to. That's where Bird and Bumble comes in. We are connecting local artisan food businesses with people who want great food. Delivered to your door without any hassle, we provide an online platform supporting both small businesses and local foodies. Whether it's a weekly treat or a special occasion, you can find delicious products that were made with care and feel great about the fact that your purchase helps both small businesses and the environment."

The company launched in December 2012 and Skye has embraced support to help her get going.

"I feel very fortunate to have realised my desire to start a business while pursuing a degree in politics at UCL. I contacted the entrepreneurship section of the university, UCL Advances, and found out they offered business advice from experienced mentors as well as free office space in their 'hatchery'. I was able to meet with an advisor who helped me to iron out my business plan and apply for a graduate entrepreneur visa. The support they offer is incredible and I'm so grateful for all their help. I also spoke to colleagues of mine from StartUp Britain, an organisation that I had interned with over the summer, and was given enormous amounts of support, advice and contacts. None of this would have been possible without them!"

Skye is spreading word of her new venture, particularly through networking.

"Contacts are so important and I learn something from everyone I meet. Talking to individuals from different industries really helps me to understand my own target market. Social media is important and by having an easily accessible website and brand we're able to attract more customers."

It's early days for Bird and Bumble but Skye is setting her sights on ambitious expansion.

"In the next 12 months we plan to significantly expand our customer base, further develop our marketing strategy, develop partnerships with delivery companies and work on wholesale orders. We are planning to open our first shop, with international expansion to follow shortly after. We have big plans for this small business!"

- www.birdandbumble.com | @skyebird

Accelerate!

And finally . . . if you want to give your business an extra injection and growth spurt, check out some of the 'Accelerators' launched by companies to give you space, funding and access to mentors, technology and customers.

- Wayra | wayra.org/en
- School for Creative Startups | www.schoolforcreativestartups.com
- Iris Ventures | www.irisnation.com/irisnews/uk_europe/iris-launches-business-incubator-iris-ventures
- Accelerator Academy | www.acceleratoracademy.com
- New Entrepreneurs Foundation | www.newentrepreneursfoundation.co.uk
- Entrepreneur First | www.entrepreneurfirst.org.uk
- Springboard | www.springboard.com
- Microsoft BizSpark | www.microsoft.com/BizSpark
- GrowthAccelerator | www.growthaccelerator.com

Nick Russell accelerated his own business by joining the Springboard programme . . .

CASE STUDY

NAME: **Nick Russell** | BUSINESS: **We Are Pop Up**

Before starting his own business, Nick Russell was a sustainability and energy consultant for multinational organisations in the UK, Europe and China. It was whilst travelling that he came up with the idea for an online platform that would help businesses arrange a temporary retail (or 'PopUp') presence, locating available spaces from landlords with vacancies on offer and helping the businesses to promote themselves when set-up.

"I was sitting in Shenzhen airport, delayed by a typhoon, and writing out business ideas to pass the time. Nine months later, I mentioned this idea to a mate. It would be a software app called The Pop Spot that enabled businesses to run PopUps and raise profile amongst potential customers. 'That's not an app,' he said, 'that's a business!' Two other friends helped shape the idea and we began planning the first execution. A month later, we had a business up and running."

Nick's three other founders came from diverse backgrounds and brought with them a range of skills: one is a computer scientist, one is a fine art painter and one is a finance consultant.

"Our experiences may be different but we share the common values of self-determination and a desire to create jobs. The relationship works because each founder has a specific area of expertise and thus has full ownership over a particular area of the business. Both individually and together we had explored a variety of entrepreneurial ideas and opportunities before creating We Are Pop Up."

The mission of We Are Pop Up is to match owners who have property to tenants who have a use for the space. At the core of the business is an online software platform where small businesses and large brands can locate PopUp shops and venues.

The business was registered in May 2012. Two months later it joined the Springboard Mobile programme, a business accelerator.

"Over the course of 12 weeks, we have seen 150 mentors from a variety of backgrounds, ranging from corporate leaders to venture capitalists. Those mentors have helped us narrow and focus the initial product offer and go-to-market strategy. We're using the 'lean start-up' process of testing the market with a minimum viable product. Through fast iterations, we have developed both a product ready for testing, as well as a highly focused company."

Springboard finishes with demonstration days in London, New York City and Silicon Valley, with the goal of closing commercial agreements and additional investment.

The business is promoting itself through hosting a monthly PUMU (Pop Up Meet Up) for evangelists from the London PopUp community, via social media (primarily Twitter, Pinterest and Facebook) and traditional sales relationships.

"We are working on demonstration projects with five different organisations in London, ranging from large commercial landlords to two start-ups at the cutting edge of retail innovation. Based on their success, we will open the platform to the commercial property sector and test the capabilities of the brand and platform to bring new businesses into the UK from outside markets."

There's plenty of activity to come, and thanks to the Springboard Accelerator Programme, this is a team that has a strong foundation and powerful network already in place.

- **www.wearepopup.com** | @wearepopup

THE BEST OF LUCK

You've read the stories, devoured the tips and completed the templates. It's time to take your own idea, passion, hobby or skill, and turn it into a business.

I hope what you've picked up from this kit is that regardless of your age, background or sector, if you're starting out as your own boss there's support all around. In whichever direction you turn, you'll find people to cheer you along and answer your questions; you'll find loans on offer and resources on tap.

Make the most of this support and never be afraid to seek help or approach mentors. With guidance from those who've trodden the entrepreneurial path, you will find your own way and build a future that offers financial reward and freedom in your working life.

Many times in 2012 I exclaimed that "start-ups are the new rock stars" – I see no sign of this wearing out and think you'll continue to be the popular kid on the block in 2013! Big companies want to be seen alongside you and customers want to buy from you. These are good conditions in which to start a new venture.

So, now it's over to you. And even though this farewell is entitled 'Best of Luck', one of my favourite quotes is one that's well known and came from golf pro Gary Player, who said: "The harder I practise, the luckier I get."

My advice to you: go practise and get lucky!

EMMA JONES | @EMMALJONES

HOW ENTERPRISE NATION CAN HELP

Enterprise Nation provides support for UK homegrown businesses through its books, events and on its website.

Whether you're dreaming of becoming your own boss, turning a talent into a business or taking over the world from your kitchen table, Enterprise Nation can help.

There's lots of free business advice on our website, events where you can learn about starting up or 'going global', and books for any kind of business in our bookshop. We can even help you with your marketing. Add your business – whatever stage it's at – to our free business directory, and we'll help you get found on the web.

Become a premium member and get even more for your business, including free eBooks, discounted tickets to events, and more ways to promote your business. Find out more at **www.enterprisenation.com**.

IN THE KIT

Readers can become premium members of Enterprise Nation for just £10 per year (half the normal price), and that includes one free business eBook per month and 25% off business events. Find out more at **www.enterprisenation.com/premium** – and make sure you activate your kit to redeem your half-price offer.

WITH THANKS

To the following people who have contributed their expertise, story or tip in the compilation of this kit:

The start-ups

Richard Baldock | **Desktag**

James Boon | **Elephant Branded**

Neil Brewster | **Lightning Apps**

Edoardo Cannarsa | **MyEdo**

Alain Desmier | **OrSaveIt**

Louise Doyle | **MESMA**

Sally Guyer | **Cambridge Raincoat Company**

Rob and Paul Forkan | **Gandys**

Donnie Maclean | **Eat Balanced**

Magdalena Marsden | **Cocoa & Heart**

Clippy McKenna | **Clippy's**

Elena Mingas | **Tangle Dress Design**

Obi Nwosu | **CLICLOC London**

Matthew Ogston | **JobPage**

MaryAnn Richardson | **MaryAnn Richardson**

Skye Robertson | **Bird and Bumble**

Nick Russell | **We Are Pop Up**

Alyssa Williamson | **Peach Blossom**

Experts

Emily Coltman | **FreeAgent**

John Hayes | **iContact**

Katie McPhee | **Eventbrite**

Laura Rigney | **Pitcher House**

Mark Shaw | **Twitter expert**

Greg Simpson | **Press For Attention**

Jackie Wade | **Winning Sales**

Dan Wilson | **Tamebay**

Joanna Tall | **Off To See My Lawyer**

Andy Yates | **Angel investor**

Enterprise Nation

San Sharma

Myles Hunt

Simon Wicks

Louise Hinchen

Chris Read

Chris Parker

IV. OFFERS & PARTNERS

HOW TO ACCESS YOUR OFFERS

To take advantage of the offers detailed in this section and many more besides, head to:

www.enterprisenation.com/startupkit2013

Enter the code below, select the individual offers you want, and you'll be shown the links and offer codes you need.

You don't have to access all the offers at once if you don't want to; you can come back at any time.

We'll be adding new offers throughout the year and you'll be able to access those too.

ACCESS CODE: supk13

ALIBABA.COM

Alibaba.com is a global e-commerce platform for small businesses operated by Alibaba.com International. The platform provides an online space that brings together buyers and sellers to communicate, collaborate and carry out global trade, helping small businesses worldwide expand to overseas markets. More than 1.4 million British SMEs are currently members of Alibaba.com.

Alibaba.com was established in 1999 by Jack Ma, a former English teacher from Hangzhou, China, and 17 other founders with a dream to help SMEs grow their business through the internet. Originally it was founded as a trading platform to help small manufacturers in China sell their wares. Since then, Alibaba.com has grown into a global online marketplace for small companies around the world to identify potential trading partners and interact with each other to conduct business online.

Alibaba.com has 29.4 million registered users from more than 240 countries and regions and showcases 2.5 million supplier storefronts. Alibaba.com International has offices across Greater China, India, Japan, Korea, the U.K. and the U.S.

Alibaba.com will be offering a new service, Verified Membership, to new and existing members in the UK, free for a limited time. The Verified Membership programme is aimed at helping suppliers establish trust with potential international buyers. Suppliers participating in this programme will undergo basic background checks to confirm that they are legitimate businesses, giving potential buyers much more confidence in doing business with them. Those who successfully pass the verification process will gain a special logo on their Alibaba.com profiles and enjoy significantly higher search rankings for their products than free members.

Join now to get higher search rankings for your business, meaning greater visibility for your products to an international audience of 29.4 million. To build trust with potential international buyers of your products/services, you just need to follow a few simple steps:

Go to www.alibaba.com/vm to initiate the Verified Member registration process. Existing members simply log-in and follow the instructions. For new members, first sign-up for a free account with Alibaba.com and during the registration process, tick the "Apply for Free Company Verification" and follow the simple instructions. Once the background verification checks are complete, your account will be awarded Verified Membership status, giving you an increase in buyer inquiries and higher visibility around the world.

www.alibaba.com

Founded in 2000 with one site, Bizspace has now been providing flexible, affordable business accommodation to both the SME and corporate markets for 12 years and has grown to 110 locations in both England and Scotland.

Bizspace provides the easiest, most flexible and cost-effective way to occupy business premises in the UK.

Finding ideal business premises for your organisation can be difficult, but with over 7m sq ft on 110 sites, Bizspace will be able to provide the right commercial units, offices, studio space, industrial premises or simple storage solution for your specific business requirements.

In order to help you start and grow your business, Bizspace are offering one month's free virtual office or one month free in any of their units, dependent on a six-month signed agreement.

www.bizspace.co.uk

COMPANIES MADE SIMPLE

Companies Made Simple are part of The Made Simple Group, specialists in start-up and small business services. They are an award-winning company formation agent founded in 2003 by Howard Graham. Specialists in the formation of UK limited companies, they have now formed over 250,000 companies.

As the name suggests, they pride themselves in the simplicity of their company formation process that allows both seasoned accountants and first-time directors (and anyone in between) to form a company within just three working hours.

Companies Made Simple are proud to offer:

- three-hour company formation
- free unlimited support
- company admin portal to manage your company
- fast-track bank account with cashback
- free domain name.

Formation happens fast so you can apply online and be in business on the same day.

Form a company for £16.99 with the simplest company formation agent!

www.companiesmadesimple.com

FreeAgent is one of the top online accounting systems available to start-ups, small businesses and freelancers both in the UK and overseas.

With FreeAgent's award-winning software you can:

- send professional invoices and automatically chase payments
- forecast tax commitments
- import bank statements and sort transactions
- manage expenses
- send estimates
- view real-time cash flow and profit & loss position
- submit VAT returns direct to HMRC
- automatically import data from your PayPal.

FreeAgent are extending a special offer in *The StartUp Kit* which gives you six months free trial plus 10% off subscriptions to their great online accounting system.

www.freeagent.com

QuickBooks is the UK's No1 Accounting Software for small business. With no accounting knowledge necessary, QuickBooks easily organises everything in one place and saves you time on everyday bookkeeping tasks. With QuickBooks you can:

- easily create and personalise invoices

- monitor cash flow and keep on top of receivables

- file your VAT returns directly to HMRC – QuickBooks is always compliant with HMRC

- get the information you need with easy-to-use reports.

Getting started is a breeze too! You can quickly import you data from an Excel spreadsheet, and follow QuickBooks' guided set up – with step-by-step tutorials and coaching tips along the way.

Get started today and immediately begin to save time on your books, so you can focus on running your business – what really matters.

Call 0808 168 4256 today and we'll give you:

- 30 day free trial

- 20% saving on your software of choice

- 60-day money-back guarantee

That's a total saving of £103!

Quote "StartUp" and be up and running in minutes!

www.intuit.co.uk

moo.com

50 free* Business Cards from moo.com

MOO is an award-winning digital printer with a difference. We make Business Cards, MiniCards, Postcards, Stickers and more – and we use premium quality paper as standard.

How is MOO different? Good question! We invented Printfinity, a unique technology that allows you to have a different image on every single card in a pack. It's a great way for new businesses to show off their work – upload product images or info and you can always carry your portfolio in your pocket. Or, choose from our exclusive range of MOO designs.

MOO offer short print runs (as few as 50 cards) so you can experiment with your cards in an affordable way, as well as avoiding waste. It's perfect for startups who still haven't decided on the perfect branding, or ecommerce companies using Printfinity as a product portfolio, with a constantly-rotating range of products.

www.moo.com

*visit moo.com/en-startupkit to claim your free pack, excluding P&P

oDesk (www.oDesk.com) is where savvy businesses and talented contractors work together on demand, without geographic limits.

As the world's largest online workplace, oDesk gives businesses the flexibility to hire on their own terms and contractors the freedom to work where they want, when they want. More than 495,000 clients and 2.5 million contractors are registered on oDesk.

How oDesk Works

Hire on demand – build a flexible workforce based on skills, ratings, and reviews.

Manage the work – see work-in-progress snapshots, time sheets, and daily logs.

Pay with ease – rest assured with safe global payments and the oDesk guarantee.

Overview of oDesk Offer

To support UK entrepreneurs as they build their businesses, oDesk is offering free work credits and our Hire Up recruiting services to *StartUp Kit* readers ($250 in offer value).

oDesk credits – *StartUp Kit* readers will receive $50 in oDesk Credits to hire online contractors.

Recruiting services – Experienced oDesk recruiters will help find the perfect contractor for your first job. Our expert talent scouts will:

- find, screen and present up to five qualified contractors for the project
- get you up and running using oDesk's online work tools
- answer questions and provide one-on-one support.

Normally $200, our Hire Up recruiting service is free to *StartUp Kit* readers!

www.odesk.com

PayPal

PayPal is a fast and secure way for customers to pay you online using all major debit and credit cards, as well as online bank transfers and PayPal balance. Customers don't even need a PayPal account to pay you.

With 26 million accounts in the UK and over 230 million worldwide, PayPal is a popular payment method with millions of online shoppers and one of the global leaders in online payments.

PayPal offers a range of products to suit your business needs and size. Whether you want to accept payments directly on your site (Website Payments Standard), through a hosted PayPal page (Website Payments Pro), over the phone (Virtual Terminal) or via email (Email Payments), PayPal has a solution to meet your needs. Benefits include:

- no set-up or monthly fees – you only start paying when you start selling
- no approval required – start accepting online payments today
- chargeback protection on qualifying transactions
- you manage the entire customer relationship: customers return to your site to confirm payment, giving you another opportunity to engage them and encourage repeat business.

PayPal is the perfect solution for businesses in a wide range of industries, which will boost sales and expand your business.

www.paypal.co.uk

EKMPOWERSHOP.COM

ekmPowershop.com is the nation's leading ecommerce provider, powering one in every five online shops in the UK.

Clients using their market-leading ecommerce solution range from multinationals like PGA Golf, Michelin Tyres, Lotus Cars and O2 – through to independent retailers and tens of thousands of SMEs.

Online based with no technical knowledge or software required, ekmPowershop.com makes it easy for any business to set up and run an online shop.

Choose from a huge selection of stunning templates – and add your own logo, colour scheme and branding to make the shop front your own. Should you require a bespoke look and feel, ekmPowershop.com's also fully customisable.

ekmPowershop.com is fully integrated with PayPal's leading payment solution, meaning you can offer customers the most popular payment methods on the internet, all on your very own online shop.

With free support and no minimum term agreement, ekmPowershop.com really is the quickest and easiest way to set up your own online shop. There's no downloads or installation to worry about – all you need is an internet connection and some products to sell!

As part of the *StartUp Kit*, PayPal and EKM are offering £1 for the first three months, to launch your complete ecommerce solution with no PayPal fees for 30 days. Once the three months expires, you pay only £19.99 per month with no contract.

www.ekmpowershop.com

Regus provides modern, flexible workspace that frees businesses of all sizes, all over the world, to work more effectively. Companies can take a fully-equipped office, desks to use part-time, come in to touch base or take advantage of a range of virtual office services.

Ready-to go: offices, meeting rooms and business lounges; the largest network of video communication studios in the world; reception facilities, virtual offices and a whole host of other business services. However you use Regus, you can get all the support a start-up or growing business needs.

That's space when you need it – but only when you need it; the room to expand as your business grows, with another fully-equipped office available overnight; elegant rooms for client meetings; a prestigious address and all the support that a business needs.

As part of their commitment to supporting small businesses, Regus are offering a great value **business start-up package** with savings of up to **£1,000**. The package includes an impressive business address, call answering and mail-handling services, professional business mentoring, business support services and discounts on meeting rooms. In addition, take advantage of access to drop-in business lounges offering an excellent place to meet and work with free Wi-Fi and tea/coffee.

www.regus.co.uk

Notes

Notes

Notes

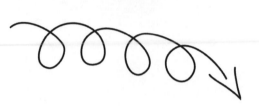

Notes

Notes